Better Homes and Gardens®

A Cross-Stitch
CHRISTMAS®

The Season for Stitching

This book belongs to:

Better Homes and Gardens®
Des Moines, Iowa

Better Homes and Gardens®
A Cross-Stitch
CHRISTMAS ®

Editor-in-Chief *Beverly Rivers*
Managing Editor **Art Director**
Julie Burch Keith *Patricia Church Podlasek*

A Cross-Stitch Christmas® Editor *Eve Mahr*
Assistant Art Director *Melissa Gansen*

Cross-Stitch & Needlework® Editor *Nancy Wyatt*
Assistant Art Director *Cherie DeTolve-Dale*
Associate Editor/Crafts Group *Barbara Hickey*
Editorial Assistant *Mary Johnson*

Contributing Photo Stylist *Jim Williams*
Illustrators *Chris Neubauer Graphics* *Glenda Aldrich*

V. P., Publishing Director *Jerry Ward*
Publisher *William R. Reed*
Advertising/Marketing Director *Maureen Ruth*
Business Manager *Janet Donnelly*
Marketing Manager *Andre Okolowitz*
Promotion Supervisor *M. Max Wilker*

Meredith CORPORATION

Chairman and CEO *William T. Kerr*

Chairman of the Executive Committee
E.T. Meredith III

Meredith Publishing Group
Publishing Group President *Christopher M. Little*
Strategic Marketing *Bill Murphy*
Finance *Max Runciman*
Circulation *Hal Oringer*
Operations *Dean Pieters*

Member

HOBBY INDUSTRY
ASSOCIATION

Our "Mark of Excellence" seal
assures you that every project in
this publication has been
constructed and checked under
the direction of the crafts experts
at Better Homes and Gardens®
Cross Stitch & Needlework®
magazine.

For book editorial questions, write
Better Homes and Gardens®
Cross Stitch & Needlework®,
1716 Locust St.–GA 311,
Des Moines, IA 50309-3023;
phone 515/284-3623; fax 515/284-3884.

ISSN: 1081-468X
ISBN: 0-696-20887-3

CHRISTMAS IS A TIME OF DREAMS

At Christmas, more than any other time of the year, we strive for perfection, working to realize our image of a flawless holiday. From the gifts we give to the arrangement of ornaments on the tree, everything must be just right. Cross-stitchers express their yuletide idealism by trimming their homes with endearing hand-made decorations and by giving lovingly stitched gifts.

This cross-stitch collection was created to fulfill your holiday stitching fantasies and make this the best Christmas ever. Whether you're a novice or a longtime stitcher, there's something for you—challenging seasonal symbols and quick-to-stitch ornaments; elegant linens and whimsical wall hangings; reverent icons of faith and lighthearted winter emblems; fun-to-wear garments and glamorous gifts.

May all your dreams for this yuletide come true. And may the pages of this book help you to fill your holidays with the bounty of The Season for Stitching.

CONTENTS

SAMPLE THE SEASON

6

*From the awe of
the Nativity to the
enjoyment of holiday
sweets, the many
joys of Christmas
are portrayed
in cross-stitch.*

AT HOME FOR CHRISTMAS

26

*Decorating for
the yule season is
steeped in tradition
and includes stockings,
afghans, and linens.*

TREASURED TREE TRIMS

50

*This collection of
adornments adds
holiday pizazz to
wreaths, centerpieces,
packages, pretty
bottles—and, of
course, the
Christmas tree.*

DRESSED FOR THE HOLIDAYS

Clothe yourself in a stylish yuletide garment! Adorn a jumper, sweater, vest, blouse, or apron with festive cross-stitch flair.

STITCHED FOR GIVING

What is more appreciated than a handmade Christmas gift? Create a memorable present that's treasured because there's love in every stitch.

CHRISTMAS CHARACTERS

Stitch the beloved personalities of Christmas—Santa, elves, nutcrackers, reindeer, snowmen, angels, and doves— to brighten your holiday home.

Sample
THE SEASON

The images of Christmas—from the solemn presence of the Christ Child to the whimsy of Santa Claus— stir our emotions and evoke the aura of the season. Preserve these visions of Christmas in cross-stitch and they become treasures for the years to come. This resplendent assortment of holiday treats captures the aromas and flavors of the season. It's stitched on 28-count Brittney fabric and embellished with sparkly beads and lacy backstitching. Complete instructions begin on page 13.

Design: Anne Cook, adapted by Barbara Sestok

SAMPLE THE SEASON

Poised against a rose-colored sky, this handsome Santa appears ready to begin his beneficent rounds through a snow-covered village. Inspired by a limited-edition statuette, below, *that was created exclusively for this book, the piece lends a timeless feel to any holiday setting. Complete instructions begin on* page 16.

Design: Adapted by Barbara Sestok from a Walnut Ridge Collectible

SAMPLE THE SEASON

Capture the heart of the holiday, the birth of the baby Jesus. The simplicity of this Nativity scene, below, *echoes the innocence of the first Christmas. It features soft shadows formed by half cross-stitches.*

Dressed in richly colored robes and embellished with stars, the stately Santa Claus at right *resembles woodcut portraits of Saint Nicholas, his 4th-century ancestor. Complete instructions for both projects begin on* page 16.

Designs: Nativity, Carol Emmer; Santa, Barbara Sestok

Carols speak the language of Christmas in music. Each of these simple samplers breathes life into the words for a well-known holiday refrain. Stitch one or all three with flower and hand-dyed threads for a one-of-a-kind look. Complete instructions begin on page 16.

Designs: Louise Young

TREATS FOR A SWEET SEASON

As shown on pages 6–7.

Fabric and Thread

14×18" piece of 28-count Cream Brittney fabric
Cotton embroidery floss in the colors listed in the key, *right*
Two additional skeins of Light old gold (DMC 676)
Four additional skeins of Blue-green (DMC 500)
Kreinik blending filament in the colors listed in the key, *right*

Supplies

Needle
Needlework frame
Mill Hill petite glass beads in the colors listed in the key, *right*
Desired frame

Instructions

Zigzag-stitch or overcast the edges of the fabric to prevent fraying. Find the center of the chart, *pages 14–15*, and the center of the fabric; begin stitching there. Use three plies of floss to work the cross-stitches over two threads of the fabric. Work the blended-needle stitches as specified in the key. Work the half cross-stitches and blended-needle half cross-stitches as specified and in the direction of the symbol. Use one ply of floss to work the backstitches unless otherwise specified in the key. Work the straight stitches using one ply of floss. Work the French knots using one ply of floss wrapped twice around the needle. Use one ply of floss to work the lazy daisy stitches. Attach the petite beads using one ply of matching floss.

Place the finished stitchery face down on a soft towel and carefully press from the back. Frame the piece as desired.

TREATS FOR A SWEET SEASON

Anchor		DMC	
002	·	000	White
897	◉	221	Shell pink
100	⊞	327	Deep antique violet
1025	♥	347	Deep salmon
009	╱	352	Coral
008	✴	353	Dark peach
683	◎	500	Blue-green
212	▲	561	Dark seafoam
210	◉	562	Medium seafoam
206	⊟	564	Light seafoam
891	◣	676	Light old gold
886	∟	677	Pale old gold
226	△	702	Christmas green
238	✕	703	Chartreuse
305	☆	725	Topaz
890	▢	729	Medium old gold
303	⊞	742	Tangerine
301	‖	744	Medium yellow
234	S	762	Pearl gray
176	⊕	793	Cornflower blue
390	∧	822	Beige-gray
850	▨	926	Gray-blue
1034	◮	931	Medium antique blue
381	◆	938	Coffee brown
1011	▯	948	Light peach
316	◈	971	Pumpkin
871	▷	3041	Medium antique violet
870	◘	3042	Light antique violet
1024	✤	3328	Dark salmon
264	♡	3348	Yellow-green
120	:	3747	Periwinkle
1032	▽	3752	Light antique blue
363	∿	3827	Golden brown
890	★	3829	Deep old gold

BLENDED NEEDLE

002	▢	000 White (2X) and 100HL Kreinik White blending filament (1X)
310 890	◗	434 Chestnut (1X) and 3829 Deep old gold (1X)
206	◇	564 Light seafoam (2X) and 100HL Kreinik White blending filament (1X)
271	⊟	819 Pink (2X) and 100HL Kreinik White blending filament (1X)
386	⊞	3823 Pale yellow (2X) and 100HL Kreinik White blending filament (1X)

HALF CROSS-STITCH

891	╱	676 Light old gold – border (2X)
886	╱	677 Pale old gold – steam (1X)
850	╱	926 Gray-blue – steam and cup (1X)

BLENDED HALF CROSS-STITCH

002	╱	000 White (2X) and 100HL Kreinik White blending filament (1X) – cup

Anchor		DMC	

BACKSTITCH

1025	╱	347 Deep salmon – cup and cupcake (1X)
310	╱	434 Chestnut – apple stem (1X)
210	╱	562 Medium seafoam – chocolate candy (1X)
1024	╱	3328 Dark salmon – chocolate candy (1X)
683	╱	500 Blue-green – details on candy wrapper, border, plates, orange, scroll, doily, cup, cupcake, jar, and pie (1X)
683	╱	500 Blue-green – all remaining backstitches (2X)

STRAIGHT STITCH

002	╱	000 White – chocolate and cupcake highlights (1X)
683	╱	500 Blue-green – pine needles, pine cone, and Santa

LAZY DAISY

683	◟	500 Blue-green – doily, plates (1X)

FRENCH KNOT

1025	●	347 Deep salmon – cup
683	●	500 Blue-green – berries, cup, cupcake, border, corners, plate, Santa's eyes, and "season"

BEADS

◉	40252 Mill Hill Iris petite glass beads – chocolate candy
◉	42011 Mill Hill Victorian gold petite glass beads – chocolate candy
◉	42013 Mill Hill Red red petite glassbeads – berries on jar lid
◉	42018 Mill Hill Crystal pink petite glass beads – chocolate candy and cupcake
◉	42027 Mill Hill Champagne petite glass beads – chocolate candy

Stitch count: 130 high x 185 wide
Finished design sizes:
28-count fabric – 9¼ x 13¼ inches
32-count fabric – 8⅛ x 11½ inches
36-count fabric – 7¼ x 10¼ inches

Treats for a Sweet Season

VILLAGE SANTA
As shown on the cover and page 8.

Fabric and Thread
15×18" piece of 25-count Bone
    Lugana fabric
Cotton embroidery floss in the
    colors listed in the key, *opposite*
One additional skein each of Light
    chestnut (DMC 435) and Light
    shell gray (DMC 453); two
    additional skeins of White
Rayon floss in the color listed in
    the key, *opposite*
Kreinik 002 Gold #8 braid
Kreinik 002HL Gold
    blending filament
4 spools of Kreinik 032 Pearl
    blending filament

Supplies
Needle
Needlework frame
Mill Hill 00557 Gold seed beads
Desired frame

Instructions
Zigzag-stitch or overcast the edges of
the fabric to prevent fraying. Find the
center of the chart, *pages 18–19,* and
the center of the fabric. Use three
plies of cotton or rayon floss to work
the cross-stitches over two threads of
the fabric. Use two plies of floss to
work the half cross-stitches in the
direction of the symbol. Work the
blended-needle stitches as specified
in the key. Use two plies of floss to
work the satin stitches. Use two plies
of floss to work the lazy daisy stitches. Work the French knots using one
ply of floss wrapped once around the
needle. Work the straight stitches and
the running stitches as specified in the
key. Work the backstitches using one
ply of floss or one strand of braid
unless otherwise specified in the key.
Attach the seed beads using one ply
of matching floss.

Place the finished stitchery facedown on a soft towel and carefully
press from the back. Frame the piece
as desired.

NATIVITY
As shown on page 10.

Fabric and Thread
16×16" piece of 28-count
    Summerstraw linen fabric

Cotton embroidery floss in the
    colors listed in the key on
    page 20

Supplies
Needle
Needlework frame
Desired frame

Instructions
Zigzag-stitch or overcast the edges
of the fabric to prevent fraying. Find
the center of the chart, *pages 20–21,*
and the center of the fabric; begin
stitching there. Use two plies of
floss to work the cross-stitches over
two threads of the fabric. Work the
half cross-stitches in the direction of
the symbol using one ply of floss.
Use one ply of floss to work the
straight stitches and the backstitches. Press the finished stitchery carefully from the back. Frame the piece
as desired.

WOODCUT SANTA
As shown on page 11.

Fabric and Thread
16×20" piece of 28-count Nordic
    blue linen
Cotton embroidery floss in the
    colors listed in the key on
    page 24
Two additional skeins each of
    White and Deep coral (DMC
    817); one additional skein of
    Straw (DMC 3820)
One skein of Metallic silver floss
    (DMC 5283); two skeins of
    Metallic gold floss (DMC 5282)
White rayon embroidery floss
    (DMC 35200)
Three spools of Kreinik 032 Pearl
    blending filament

Supplies
Needle
Needlework frame
Seed beads in the colors listed in
    the key on *page 24*
Desired frame

Instructions
Zigzag-stitch or overcast the edges
of the fabric to prevent fraying. Find
the center of the chart, *pages 22–23,*
and the center of the fabric; begin
stitching there. Use three plies of
cotton floss, three plies of metallic

floss, or two plies of rayon floss to
work the cross-stitches over two
threads of the fabric. Work the
blended-needle stitches as specified
in the key. Work the backstitches
using one ply of floss unless otherwise specified in the key.

Work the straight stitches and the
blended-needle straight stitches as
specified. For the wreath trim, twist
the blended threads together before
returning the needle to the back of
the fabric. Work the French knots as
specified, wrapping the thread once
around the needle.

Refer to the diagram, *page 24,*
and use two plies of floss to work
the tassel stitches over the number
of threads indicated in the key.
Attach the seed beads using two
plies of matching floss. Place the
finished stitchery facedown on a
soft towel and carefully press from
the back. Frame the piece as desired.

CAROL SAMPLERS
As shown on page 12.

Fabric and Thread
For each mini sampler
8×7" piece of 28-count
    Sandstone linen
DMC flower thread in the colors
    listed in the key on *page 25*
Wildflowers cotton overdyed
    thread in the colors listed in
    the key on *page 25*
Waterlilies silk overdyed thread in
    the colors listed in the key
    on *page 25*

Supplies
Needle
Needlework frame
Desired frame

Instructions
Zigzag-stitch or overcast the edges
of the fabric to prevent fraying. Find
the vertical center of the chart, *page
24 or 25,* and the fabric. Measure 2"
from the top of the fabric; begin
stitching the top row of the desired
chart there. Use one strand of flower
thread,   one   strand   of   the
Wildflowers,   or   three   plies   of
Waterlilies thread to work the cross-
stitches over two threads of the
fabric. (When stitching with the
Wildflowers and Waterlilies, work

each stitch completely before proceeding to the next stitch.) Work the backstitches using one strand of flower thread or Wildflowers.

Use one strand of Wildflowers thread to work the Smyrna cross-stitches. Work the herringbone stitches using two plies of Waterlilies thread and referring to the diagram, *page 25.* Work the straight stitches and the running stitches using one strand of flower thread. Refer to the diagram, *page 25,* and use one strand of Wildflowers thread to work the star stitches over the number of threads indicated on the chart.

Press the finished stitchery carefully from the back. Frame each piece as desired.

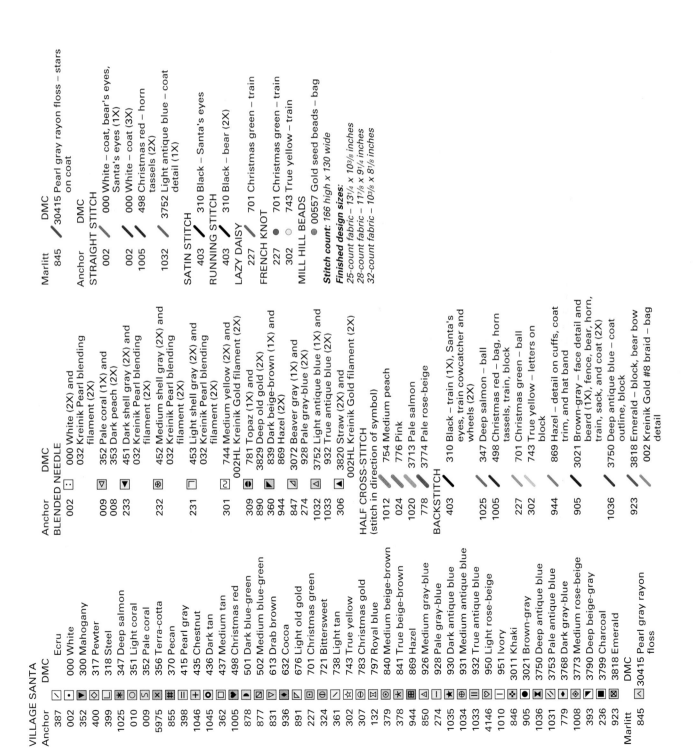

VILLAGE SANTA

Anchor	DMC
387	Ecru
002	000 White
352	300 Mahogany
400	317 Pewter
399	318 Steel
1025	347 Deep salmon
010	351 Light coral
009	352 Pale coral
5975	356 Terra-cotta
855	370 Pecan
398	415 Pearl gray
1046	435 Chestnut
1045	436 Dark tan
362	437 Medium tan
1005	498 Christmas red
878	501 Dark blue-green
877	502 Medium blue-green
831	613 Drab brown
936	632 Cocoa
891	676 Light old gold
227	701 Christmas green
324	721 Bittersweet
361	738 Light tan
302	743 True yellow
307	783 Christmas gold
132	797 Royal blue
379	840 Medium beige-brown
378	841 True beige-brown
944	869 Hazel
850	926 Medium gray-blue
274	928 Pale gray-blue
1035	930 Dark antique blue
1034	931 Medium antique blue
1033	932 True antique blue
4146	950 Light rose-beige
1010	951 Ivory
846	3011 Khaki
905	3021 Brown-gray
1036	3750 Deep antique blue
1031	3753 Pale antique blue
779	3768 Dark gray-blue
1008	3773 Medium rose-beige
393	3790 Deep beige-gray
236	3799 Charcoal
923	3818 Emerald

Marlitt	DMC
845	30415 Pearl gray rayon floss

Anchor	DMC	BLENDED NEEDLE
002	000 White (2X) and	032 Kreinik Pearl blending filament (2X)
009	352 Pale coral (1X) and	
008	353 Dark peach (2X)	
233	451 Dark shell gray (2X) and	032 Kreinik Pearl blending filament (2X)
232	452 Medium shell gray (2X) and	032 Kreinik Pearl blending filament (2X)
231	453 Light shell gray (2X) and	032 Kreinik Pearl blending filament (2X)
301	744 Medium yellow (2X) and	002HL Kreinik Gold filament (2X)
309	781 Topaz (1X) and	
890	3829 Deep old gold (2X)	
360	839 Dark beige-brown (1X) and	
944	869 Hazel (2X)	
847	3072 Beaver gray (1X) and	
274	928 Pale gray-blue (2X)	
1032	3752 Light antique blue (1X) and	
1033	932 True antique blue (2X)	
306	3820 Straw (2X) and	002HL Kreinik Gold filament (2X)

HALF CROSS-STITCH
(stitch in direction of symbol)

Anchor	DMC
1012	754 Medium peach
024	776 Pink
1020	3713 Pale salmon
778	3774 Pale rose-beige

BACKSTITCH

Anchor	DMC
403	310 Black – train (1X), Santa's eyes, train cowcatcher and wheels (2X)
1025	347 Deep salmon – ball
1005	498 Christmas red – bag, horn tassels, train, block
227	701 Christmas green – ball
302	743 True yellow – letters on block
944	869 Hazel – detail on cuffs, coat trim, and hat band
905	3021 Brown-gray – face detail and beard (1X), fence, bear, horn, train, sack, and coat (2X)
1036	3750 Deep antique blue – coat outline, block
923	3818 Emerald – block, bear bow
	002 Kreinik Gold #8 braid – bag detail

Marlitt	DMC
845	30415 Pearl gray rayon floss – stars on coat

STRAIGHT STITCH

Anchor	DMC
002	000 White – coat, bear's eyes, Santa's eyes (1X)
002	000 White – coat (3X)
1005	498 Christmas red – horn tassels (2X)
1032	3752 Light antique blue – coat detail (1X)

SATIN STITCH
403 | 310 Black – Santa's eyes

RUNNING STITCH
403 | 310 Black – bear (2X)

LAZY DAISY
227 | 701 Christmas green – train

FRENCH KNOT
227 | 701 Christmas green – train
302 | 743 True yellow – train

MILL HILL BEADS
00557 Gold seed beads – bag

Stitch count: 166 high x 130 wide
Finished design sizes:
25-count fabric – 13 1/4 x 10 3/8 inches
28-count fabric – 11 7/8 x 9 1/4 inches
32-count fabric – 10 3/8 x 8 1/8 inches

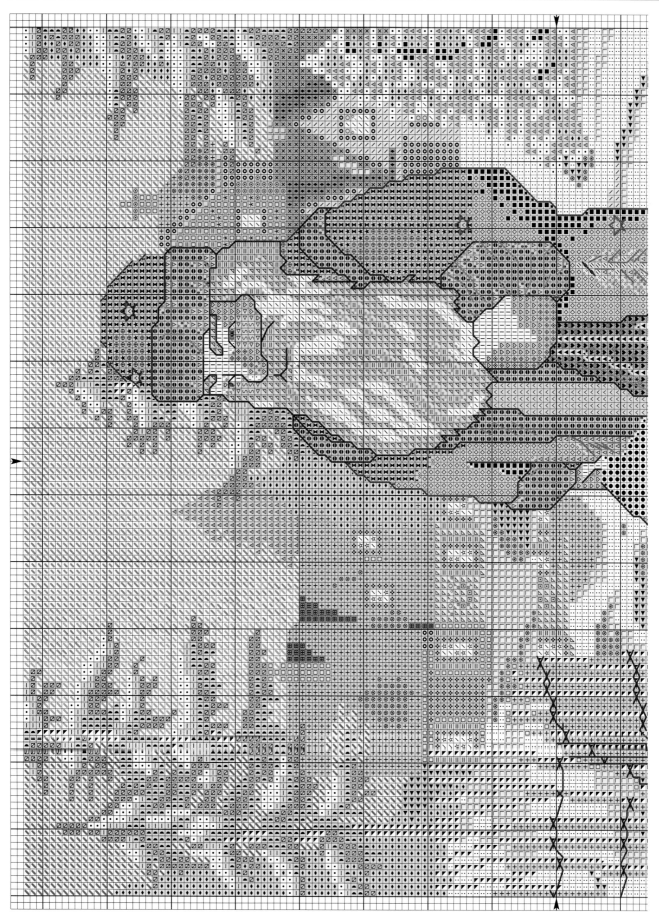

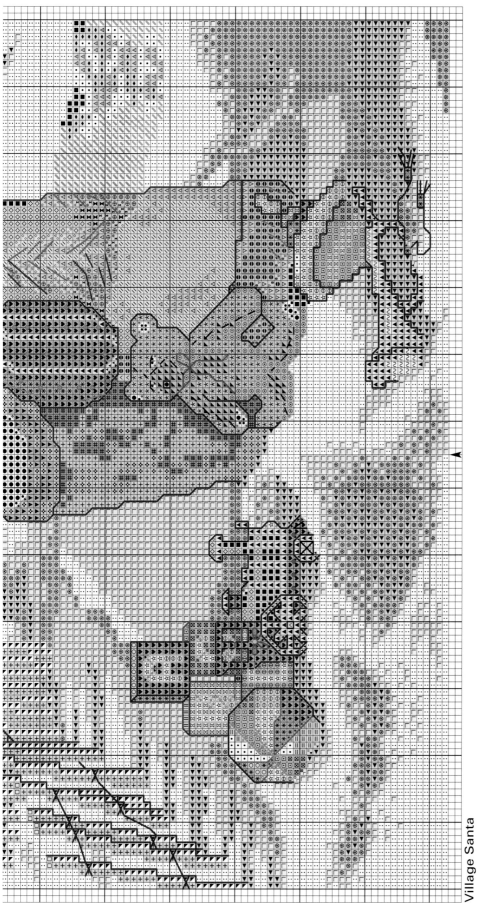

Village Santa

NATIVITY

Anchor	DMC		Anchor	DMC		Anchor	DMC
002	•	000 White	359	▶	801 Coffee brown		HALF CROSS-STITCH
399	⌐	318 Light steel	390	⌐	822 Pale beige-gray		(stitch in direction of symbol)
008	☑	353 Dark peach	944	✚	869 Dark hazel	360	╱ 3031 Mocha –
1014	▶◀	355 Dark terra-cotta	1915	◆	918 Red-copper		background (1X)
5975	✳	356 Medium terra-cotta	1035	⊞	930 Dark antique blue		**Stitch count:** *147 high x 130 wide*
401	▶◀	413 Pewter	1934	⊕	931 Medium antique blue		**Finished design sizes:**
235	★	414 Dark steel	1033	◇	932 True antique blue		*28-count fabric – 10½ x 9¼ inches*
398	—	415 Pearl-gray	861	◀	935 Pine green		*32-count fabric – 9⅛ x 8⅛ inches*
374	◣	420 Medium hazel	152	▼	939 Navy		*36-count fabric – 8⅛ x 7¼ inches*
373	⊕	422 Light hazel	1011	✚	948 Light peach		
860	#	522 Dark olive drab	360	■	3031 Mocha		
859	◪	523 Medium olive drab	888	✕	3045 Dark yellow-beige		DMC
9038	◥	640 Dark beige-gray	887	◁	3046 Medium yellow-beige	031	☐ 3708 Watermelon
392	☆	642 Medium beige-gray	886	‖	3047 Light yellow-beige	1036	● 3750 Deep antique blue
830	◁	644 Light beige-gray	883	⊙	3064 Cocoa	1009	‖ 3770 Ivory
926	○	712 Cream	263	◆	3362 Dark loden	1013	╎ 3778 True terra-cotta
882	◎	758 Light terra-cotta	262	◈	3363 Medium loden	393	◑ 3790 Deep beige-gray

BACKSTITCH

5975	╱	356 Medium terra-cotta – hands and facial details
896	╱	3721 Shell pink – Mary and shepherd's lips
360	╱	3031 Mocha – all remaining backstitches

STRAIGHT STITCH

5975	╱	356 Medium terra-cotta – infant's lips
944	╱	869 Dark hazel – shepherd, Mary, and Joseph's eyebrows

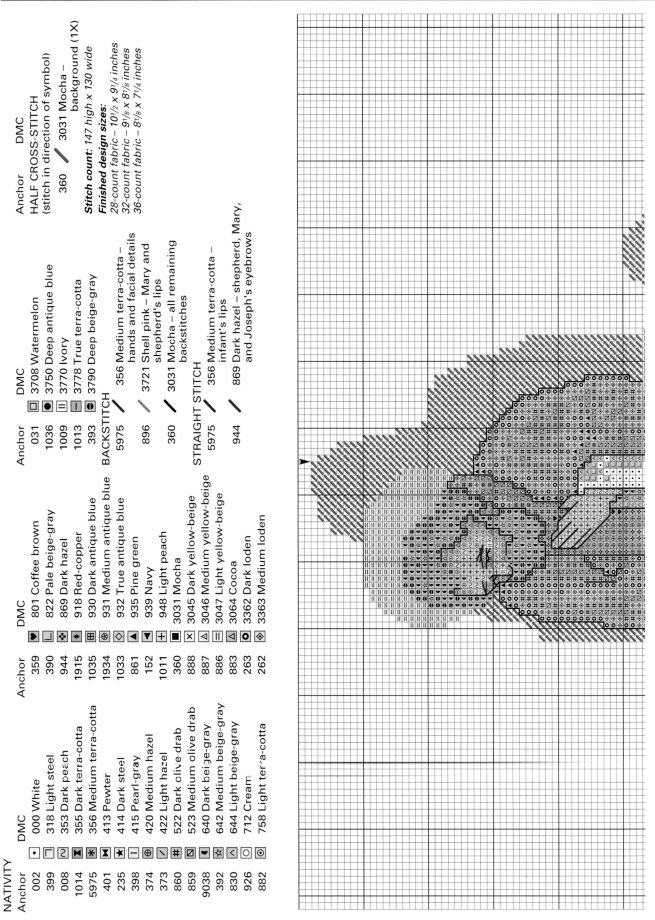

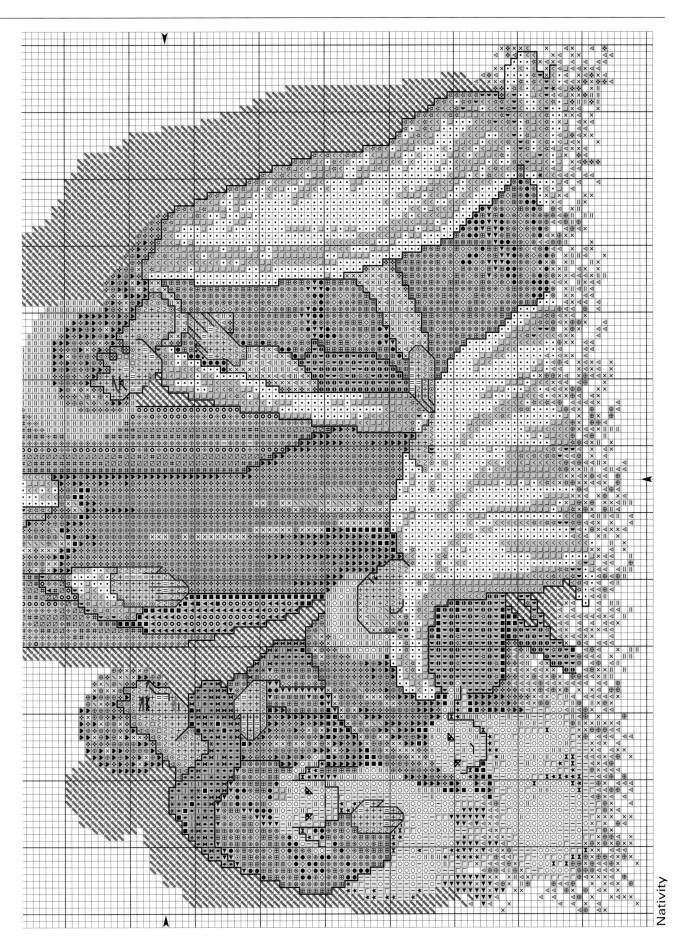

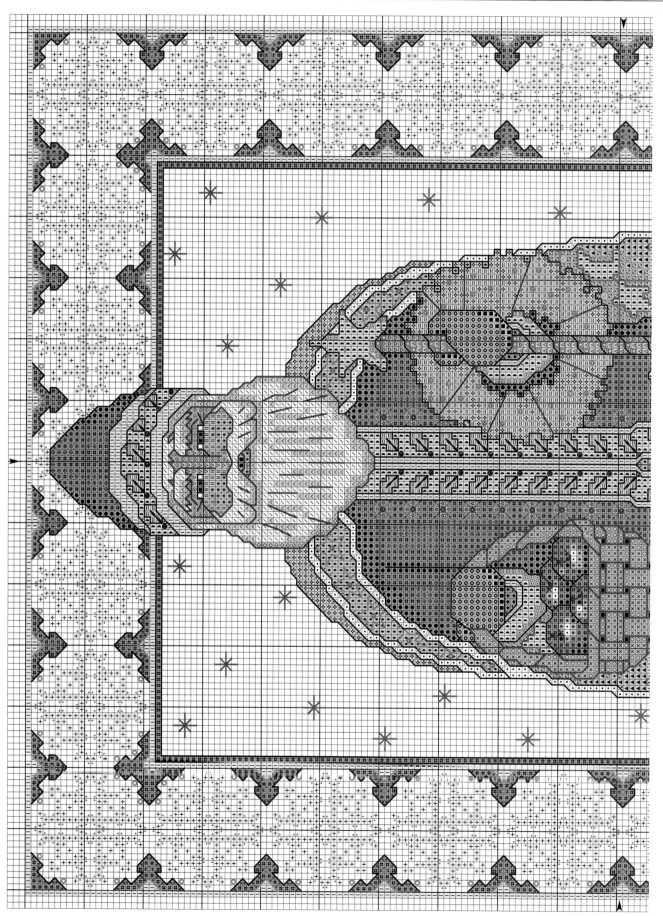

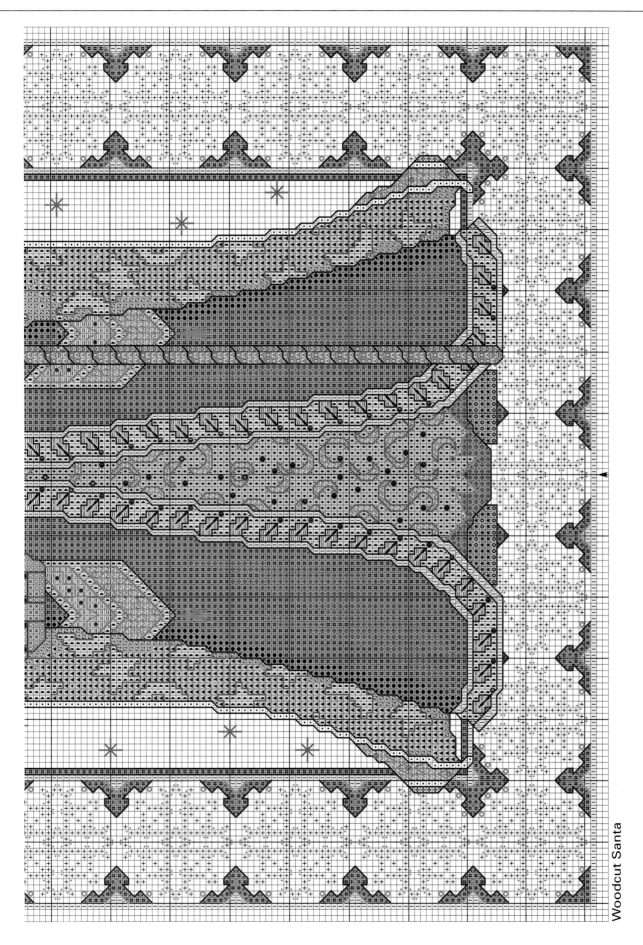

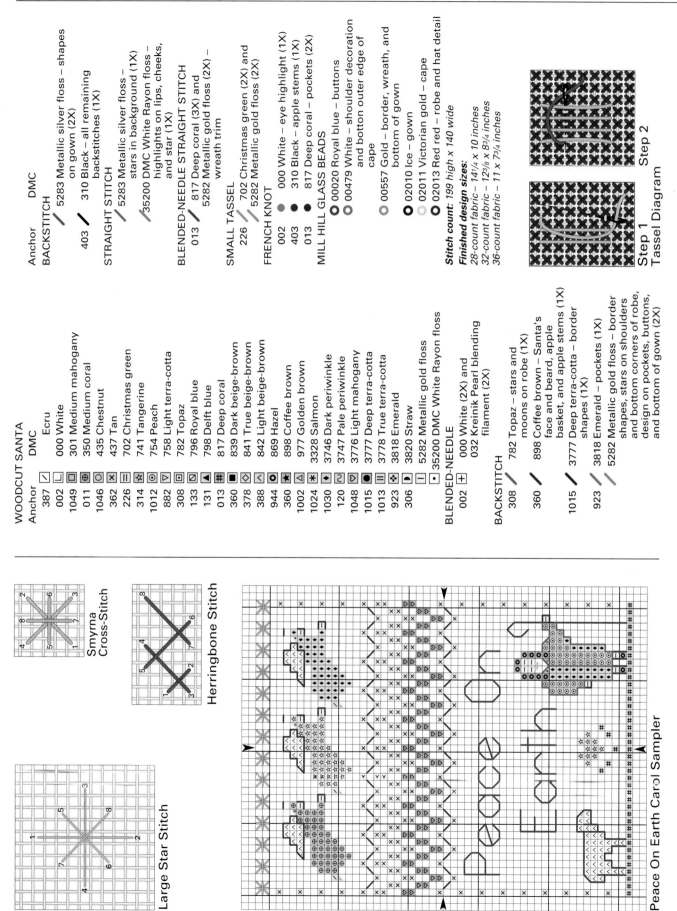

WOODCUT SANTA

Anchor	DMC	
387		Ecru
002	000	White
1049	301	Medium mahogany
011	350	Medium coral
1046	435	Chestnut
362	437	Tan
226	702	Christmas green
314	741	Tangerine
1012	754	Peach
882	758	Light terra-cotta
308	782	Topaz
133	796	Royal blue
131	798	Delft blue
013	817	Deep coral
360	839	Dark beige-brown
378	841	True beige-brown
388	842	Light beige-brown
944	869	Hazel
360	898	Coffee brown
1002	977	Golden brown
1024	3328	Salmon
1030	3746	Dark periwinkle
120	3747	Pale periwinkle
1048	3776	Light mahogany
1015	3777	Deep terra-cotta
1013	3778	True terra-cotta
923	3818	Emerald
306	3820	Straw
	5282	Metallic gold floss
	35200	DMC White Rayon floss

BLENDED-NEEDLE
002 000 White (2X) and
032 Kreinik Pearl blending filament (2X)

BACKSTITCH
308 782 Topaz – stars and moons on robe (1X)
360 898 Coffee brown – Santa's face and beard, apple basket, and apple stems (1X)
1015 3777 Deep terra-cotta – border shapes (1X)
923 3818 Emerald – pockets (1X)
5282 Metallic gold floss – border shapes, stars on shoulders and bottom corners of robe, design on pockets, buttons, and bottom of gown (2X)

Anchor DMC
BACKSTITCH
5283 Metallic silver floss – shapes on gown (2X)
403 310 Black – all remaining backstitches (1X)
STRAIGHT STITCH
5283 Metallic silver floss – stars in background (1X)
35200 DMC White Rayon floss – highlights on lips, cheeks, and star (1X)
BLENDED-NEEDLE STRAIGHT STITCH
013 817 Deep coral (3X) and
5282 Metallic gold floss (2X) – wreath trim
SMALL TASSEL
226 702 Christmas green (2X) and
5282 Metallic gold floss (2X)
FRENCH KNOT
002 000 White – eye highlight (1X)
403 310 Black – apple stems (1X)
013 817 Deep coral – pockets (2X)
MILL HILL GLASS BEADS
00020 Royal blue – buttons
00479 White – shoulder decoration and bottom outer edge of cape
00557 Gold – border, wreath, and bottom of gown
02010 Ice – gown
02011 Victorian gold – cape
02013 Red red – robe and hat detail

Stitch count: 199 high x 140 wide
Finished design sizes:
28-count fabric – 14¼ x 10 inches
32-count fabric – 12⅜ x 8¾ inches
36-count fabric – 11 x 7¾ inches

Step 1   Step 2
Tassel Diagram

Smyrna Cross-Stitch

Herringbone Stitch

Large Star Stitch

Peace On Earth Carol Sampler

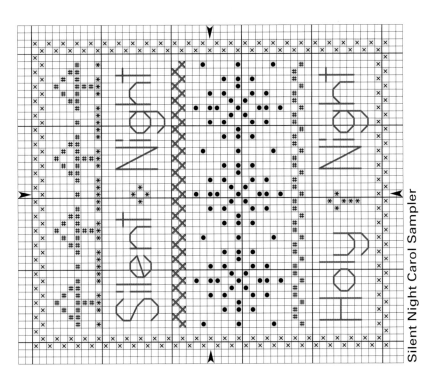

Silent Night Carol Sampler

DMC Flower Thread
HERRINGBONE STITCH
⟩⟨ 101 Caron Waterlilies Cherry
silk thread – area under
"Silent Night"

STRAIGHT STITCH
╱ 2924 Gray-blue flower thread –
top of We Three Kings

RUNNING STITCH
╱ 2433 Brown flower thread –
area below village (1X)

STAR STITCH
✳ 085 Caron Wildflowers
Antique brass – top of
We Three Kings

Peace on Earth stitch count: *54 high x 41 wide*
Peace on Earth finished design sizes:
28-count fabric – 3⅞ x 3 inches
32-count fabric – 3⅜ x 2½ inches
36-count fabric – 3 x 2¼ inches

Silent Night stitch count: *51 high x 43 wide*
Silent Night finished design sizes:
28-count fabric – 3⅝ x 3⅛ inches
32-count fabric – 3⅛ x 2⅝ inches
36-count fabric – 2⅞ x 2⅜ inches

We Three Kings stitch count: *49 high x 41 wide*
We Three Kings finished design sizes:
28-count fabric – 3½ x 3 inches
32-count fabric – 3 x 2½ inches
36-count fabric – 2¾ x 2¼ inches

We Three Kings Carol Sampler

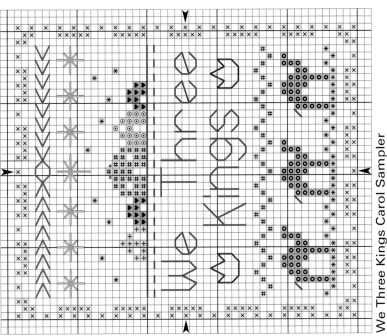

CAROL SAMPLERS
DMC Flower Thread
● 2377 Navy blue
▲ 2433 Brown
☆ 2570 Mauve
＋ 2592 Peacock blue
⊕ 2768 Blue-green
▶ 2814 Garnet
✳ 2833 Golden wheat
╱ 2929 Very dark antique blue
◆ 2930 Dark antique blue
⊙ 2931 Medium antique blue
▯ 2948 Beige

Caron Waterlilies
083 Pine forest silk thread
▷ 101 Cherry silk thread
◁ 132 Honeysuckle silk thread

DMC Flower Thread
Caron Wildflowers
☒ 008 Nefertiti

BACKSTITCH
╱ 2337 Navy blue flower thread –
lettering (1X)
╱ 2433 Brown flower thread –angels,
lamb and shepherd; camel
tails and area below village (1X)
╱ 2814 Garnet flower thread –
crowns (1X)
╱ 2929 Very dark antique blue flower
thread – shepherd's coat
╱ 008 Caron Wildflowers Nefertiti –
design (1X)

SMYRNA CROSS-STITCH
✳ 085 Caron Wildflowers
Antique brass – top of
We Three Kings (1X)

AT HOME
for CHRISTMAS

Fill your home with the warm and

welcoming spirit of Christmas—

and cross-stitch! The colorful

cardinal afghan, the joyful candy-

cane pillow, and the sledding-mice

stocking and treasure box were all

designed for you to stitch with love

and seasonal cheer. Turn the page

for a closer view of these and other

projects designed to make your

house a holiday home.

Curl up on Christmas Eve and wait for Santa under this cozy cardinal afghan. The colorful finch, perched upon a holly bough, is stitched over two threads on 14-count fabric, so each square works up quickly. Folk-art stockings brighten the mantelpiece below. *Rustico Aida gives these stockings a homespun look and copper braid adds sparkle. There's also a country blue-and-violet version shown on* pages 36–37. *Instructions for the afghan and stockings begin on* page 34.

Designs: Afghan, Barbara Sestok; Stockings, Judy Kauffman

Use these Christmas roses all season long; the blooms won't wilt. They're stitched on 16-count Aida banding so you can attach them to towels in the color and size of your choice. Complete instructions are on page 38.

Bedazzle your holiday table with a runner of glistening rayon bows with twinkling bead picots, *opposite. The elegant ribbon-and-holly motifs, positioned on a center-of-the-table oval, command attention for your beautiful stitching. Complete instructions begin on page 39.*

Designs: Barbara Sestok

A touch of whimsy keeps the holidays lighthearted. Spell out seasonal joy by stitching it in candy-cane letters. A prefinished pillow with 26-count Heatherfield center means you can stitch, stuff, and display—there's no finishing. Winter fun for woodland creatures is the theme of this personalized stocking and treasure box. Stitch both on snowy white Brittney fabric with sparkly metallic thread accents for the frosty look of a December afternoon. Complete instructions for both projects begin on page 43.

Designs: Pillow, Phyllis Dobbs; Stocking and Box, Laura Doyle

CARDINAL AFGHAN
As shown on page 28.

Fabric and Thread
Purchased 45×54" 14-count Cream Teresa afghan
Cotton embroidery floss in the colors listed in the key *below*
Two additional skeins of 704, 815, 3345, 3801, and 3819; four additional skeins of 814; six additional skeins of 905 and 3371 and ten additional skeins of 321

Supplies
Needle

Instructions
Find the center of the chart and the center of one square of the afghan; begin stitching there. Use six plies of floss to work the cross-stitches over two threads of the fabric. Work the French knots using two plies of floss wrapped once around the needle. Work the backstitches using two plies of floss. Use six plies of floss to work the running stitches. Machine-topstitch around all four sides of the afghan 3½" from the edges. For the fringe, carefully remove the threads between the topstitching and the cut edge.

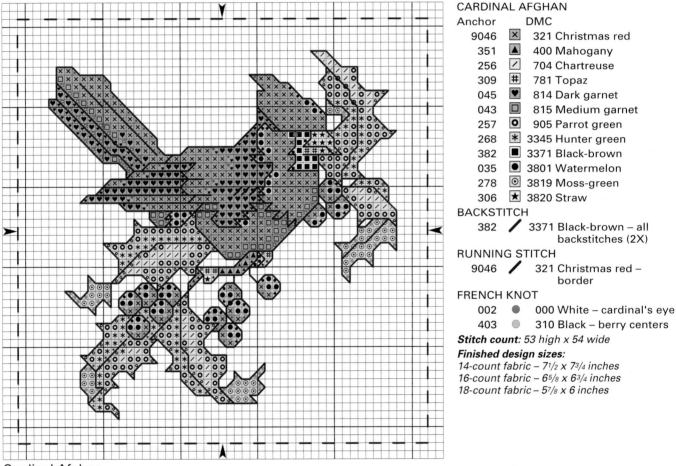

Cardinal Afghan

CARDINAL AFGHAN

Anchor		DMC	
9046	☒	321	Christmas red
351	▲	400	Mahogany
256	╱	704	Chartreuse
309	⊞	781	Topaz
045	♥	814	Dark garnet
043	☐	815	Medium garnet
257	⊙	905	Parrot green
268	✳	3345	Hunter green
382	■	3371	Black-brown
035	●	3801	Watermelon
278	◎	3819	Moss-green
306	★	3820	Straw

BACKSTITCH

382	╱	3371 Black-brown – all backstitches (2X)

RUNNING STITCH

9046	╱	321 Christmas red – border

FRENCH KNOT

002	●	000 White – cardinal's eye
403	●	310 Black – berry centers

Stitch count: *53 high x 54 wide*
Finished design sizes:
14-count fabric – 7½ x 7¾ inches
16-count fabric – 6⅝ x 6¾ inches
18-count fabric – 5⅞ x 6 inches

Stitching on Afghans

Whether you cross-stitch an afghan for yourself or as a gift, the sheer size of the project makes it impressive. Here are some suggestions to ensure that the afghan you stitch becomes a treasured heirloom.

1. Buy enough of each floss color at one time to ensure the same dye lot will be used throughout the project.

2. Even if your project instructions call for six plies of floss, separate the six-ply strand into individual plies, then recombine as the instructions specify. This will help the floss cover the fabric completely.

3. If your fabric has a raised pattern on one side, be sure to stitch on that side.

4. Use a needlework frame to help keep stitches even. Most afghan fabrics are 14 or 18 threads per inch and stitched over two threads, which means your stitches will be a little larger than on Aida or linen.

5. Afghan fabrics are not meant to be lined or backed with a fusible facing, so take some extra care to make the back side neat. Begin each thread with a loop knot (see To secure thread at the beginning, *page 124*) when the instructions call for an even number of floss plies. Other times, use a waste knot. Weave waste-knot and end-of-the-thread tails vertically through stitches on the back of the afghan fabric.

6. You'll be working with at least four plies of floss, so be careful not to twist the thread. Use a second tapestry needle, a trolley needle, or a laying tool to spread the plies into a flat ribbon just before you pull each stitch into position. This technique improves coverage.

7. Stitch the center motif first, then work outward to the border.

8. Fringe the afghan when stitching is complete.

FOLK-ART STOCKINGS

As shown on pages 29 and 36–37, the finished stockings measure 7" tall and 5¼" wide.

Fabric and Thread

For each pair of stockings
10×18" piece of 14-count Oatmeal or Horizon blue Rustico Aida cloth
9×12" piece of polyester fleece
¼ yard of coordinating print fabric for back
Cotton embroidery floss in the colors listed in the key on *page 36 or 37*
Kreinik ¹⁄₁₆" ribbon in the color listed in the key on *page 36 or 37*

Supplies

For each pair of stockings
Needle
Needlework frame
Erasable fabric marking pen
¼ yard of contrasting fabric for piping (optional)
¾ yard of ⅛"-diameter cording for side piping
½ yard of ⅛"- or ¼"-diameter cording for top piping
Sewing thread to match fabrics
10" of ⅛"-wide satin ribbon
3 additional yards ⅛"-wide satin ribbon (optional)
4×¾" piece of cardboard (optional)

Instructions

Zigzag or overcast the edges of the Aida fabric to prevent fraying. Divide the fabric into two 10×9" rectangles by folding it in half and creasing it. Find the center of one chart, *page 36 or 37,* and the center of one rectangle; begin stitching there. Use three plies of floss or one strand of ribbon to work all cross-stitches. Work backstitches using one ply of floss. For the second stocking find the center of the remaining chart and rectangle; begin stitching there.

When both stockings are stitched, press from the back. Use the erasable marking pen to draw the outline of each stocking onto the fabric as indicated by the dashed line on the chart. Cut out each stocking ½" beyond the drawn line. Use the stitched stocking as a pattern to cut two interfacing pieces from fleece and two back and four lining pieces from the print fabric.

For the piping on the sides and foot of each stocking, cut enough 1½"-wide bias strips to equal 20" from the print or contrasting fabric. For the piping at the top, cut enough 1½"-wide bias strips to equal 9" from the desired fabric.

To construct the stockings, use ½" seams. Baste a fleece interfacing to the back of each stitched stocking. For the piping, sew the short ends of the bias strips together. Center the cording lengthwise on the wrong side of the piping strip. Fold the fabric around the cording with the raw edges together. Use a zipper foot to sew through both layers near the cording. Baste the piping to the stitched stockings, matching the piping seam to the drawn lines. With right sides together, sew each stitched stocking and back together, leaving the top open. Clip the curves, turn right side out, and press. If desired, baste piping around the top of each stocking.

Stitch the lining pieces together in pairs, leaving the top and a 3" space at the bottom of the foot open. *Do not* turn. Slip a stocking inside each lining. Stitch around the top of each stocking through all layers. Turn each stocking right side out through the opening in the foot of the lining. Sew the opening in the foot closed and push the lining inside the stocking. Press well.

Cut two 5" lengths of ribbon and fold each in half. Hand-tack a loop inside the top right-hand corner of each stocking. For the bows, cut two 8" pieces of ribbon and set aside. Divide the remaining ribbon in half; wrap each half around the cardboard. Slip one 8" piece of ribbon under the loops on the cardboard and tie it firmly around them. Slide the loops off the cardboard and tack the resulting bow to the upper corner of the stocking. Repeat with the remaining ribbon.

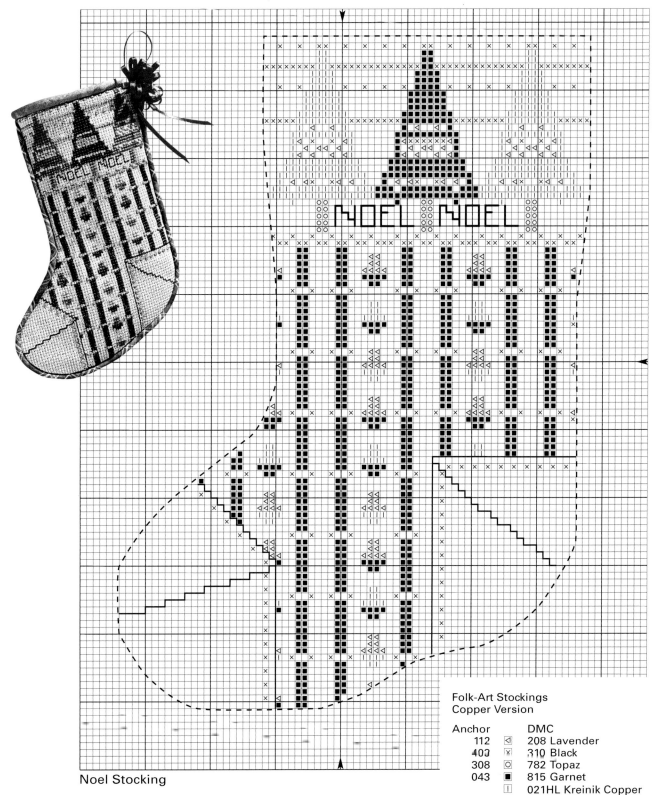

Noel Stocking

Folk-Art Stockings
Copper Version

Anchor		DMC	
112	◁	208	Lavender
403	☒	310	Black
308	○	782	Topaz
043	■	815	Garnet
	⏐	021HL Kreinik Copper ¹⁄₁₆" ribbon	

BACKSTITCH
043	╱	815 Medium garnet

Stitch count: *99 high x 72 wide*
Finished design sizes:
14-count fabric – 7 x 5⅛ inches
16-count fabric – 6⅛ x 4½ inches
18-count fabric – 5½ x 4 inches

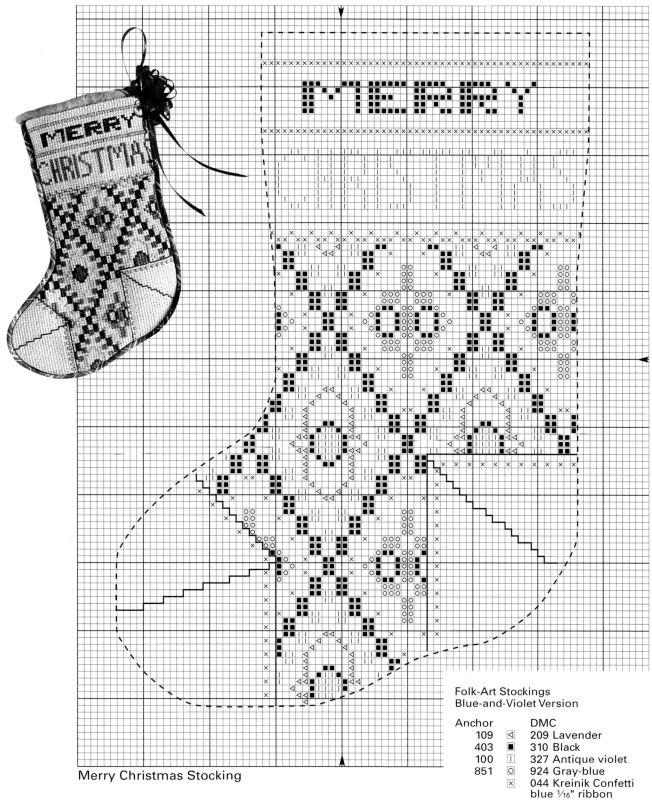

Folk-Art Stockings
Blue-and-Violet Version

Anchor		DMC
109	◁	209 Lavender
403	■	310 Black
100	⊡	327 Antique violet
851	○	924 Gray-blue
	☒	044 Kreinik Confetti blue 1/16" ribbon

BACKSTITCH
| 403 | ╱ | 310 Black |

Merry Christmas Stocking

Stitch count: 99 high x 72 wide
Finished design sizes:
14-count fabric – 7 x 5⅛ inches
16-count fabric – 6⅛ x 4½ inches
18-count fabric – 5½ x 4 inches

AT HOME FOR CHRISTMAS

CHRISTMAS ROSE TOWEL SET
As shown on page 30.

Fabric and Thread
1¾ yards of 2⅜"-wide 16-count red-and-gold Aida banding or the length needed to fit the desired towels and washcloth
Cotton embroidery floss in the colors listed in the key, *opposite*
Metallic gold embroidery floss
Purchased bath towel, hand towel, and washcloth set

Supplies
Needle
Matching sewing thread

Instructions
Measure the width of each towel and the washcloth and cut a piece of banding at least 2" wider than each measurement. (We used 15" for the washcloth, 18" for the hand towel, and 29" for the bath towel.) Zigzag-stitch or overcast the ends of the banding to prevent fraying. For each piece, find the center of the chart and the center of the banding; begin stitching there. For the towels, stitch the entire chart. For the washcloth, stitch only the area within the dashed lines. The green and gold border at the top and bottom can be extended to the ends of the banding, if desired. Use two plies of floss to work the cross-stitches. Work the backstitches using one ply of floss unless otherwise specified. Work the straight stitches using two plies of floss. Work the French knots and the blended-needle French knots as specified, wrapping the thread once around the needle. Press the stitched banding carefully from the back.

Pin the banding on the towels and washcloth as desired. Fold the banding ends under so they are even with the towel or washcloth edges. Machine-topstitch along the edges of the banding.

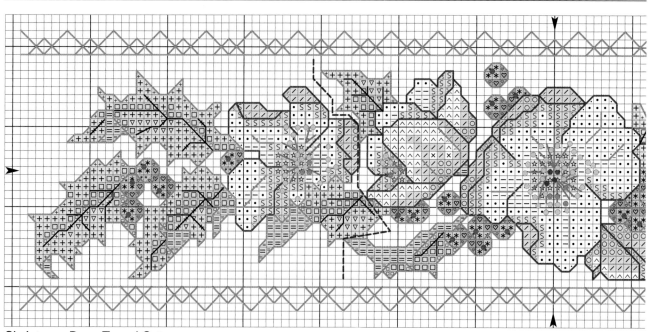

Christmas Rose Towel Set

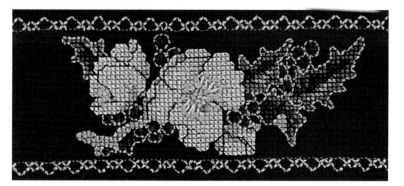

Only this center portion, *left*, of the chart should be stitched for the Christmas Rose washcloth. Dashed lines on the chart indicate the part of it that is stitched onto the washcloth's piece of banding.

RIBBONS-AND-HOLLY TABLE RUNNER

As shown on page 31, the finished table runner measures 19" wide and 38½" long.

Fabric and Thread
24×43½" piece of 25-count Christmas red Lugana fabric
Rayon embroidery floss in the colors listed in the key on *page 42*
One additional skein each of 30472, 30676, 30746, and 30976; two additional skeins of 30744; and three additional skeins of 33820

Supplies
Needle; beading needle
Needlework frame
3 packages of Mill Hill 40557 gold petite seed beads
Erasable fabric marking pen
Red sewing thread

Instructions
Zigzag-stitch or overcast the edges of the fabric to prevent fraying. Find the vertical center of the chart, *pages 40–41,* and of the fabric. Measure 2" from the edge on one end of the fabric; begin stitching there. Use two plies of floss to work the cross-stitches over two threads of the fabric. Use three plies of floss to work the satin stitches over the number of threads indicated on the chart. Work the backstitches using one ply of floss. Use one ply of floss to work the straight stitches unless otherwise specified in the key. Work the French knots using one ply of floss wrapped once around the needle. Attach the petite seed beads using one ply of matching floss. Stitch the opposite end of the table runner in the same manner. Place the finished stitchery face-down on a soft towel and carefully press from the back.

With the design centered, trim the fabric to measure 20×39½". With the erasable marking pen, draw rounded corners using a 9½" radius onto the fabric (see tip box, *page 42*). Zigzag-stitch or serge the edges of the fabric ½" beyond the marked line. Turn the edges of the fabric under ½" and hand-stitch; press.

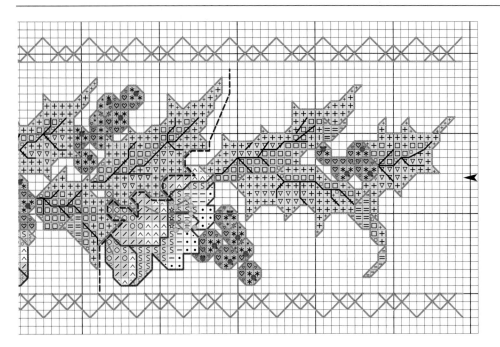

CHRISTMAS ROSE TOWEL SET

Anchor		DMC	
893	◯	224	Light shell pink
1026	╱	225	Pale shell pink
253	☆	472	Avocado
1005	▽	498	Christmas red
256	▽	704	Chartreuse
275	•	746	Off-white
035	✱	891	Carnation
257	+	905	Parrot green
847	S	3072	Beaver gray
292	−	3078	Pale lemon
268	▢	3345	Hunter green
1009	∧	3770	Ivory
278	≡	3819	Moss green

BACKSTITCH

380	╱	838 Beige-brown – flowers (1X)
257	╱	905 Parrot green – border (1X)
847	╱	3072 Beaver gray – flower detail (2X)

Anchor		DMC
BACKSTITCH

382	╱	3371 Black-brown – veins in leaves (1X)
	╱	5282 Metallic gold floss – all remaining backstitches (2X)

STRAIGHT STITCH

275	╱	746 Off-white – flower centers (2X)

FRENCH KNOT

307	●	783 Christmas gold – flower centers (2X)
906	●	829 Bronze – berries (1X)
292	●	3078 Pale lemon – flower centers (2X)

BLENDED-NEEDLE FRENCH KNOT

290	●	444 Medium lemon (1X) and
302		743 Yellow (1X) – flower centers

Stitch count: 35 high x 138 wide
Finished design sizes:
16-count fabric – 2⅛ x 8⅝ inches
14-count fabric – 2½ x 9⅞ inches

Ribbons-and-Holly Table Runner

RIBBONS-AND-HOLLY TABLE RUNNER

Marlitt	DMC		DMC Rayon	
253	472	⊟	30472	Avocado
281	580	◎	30580	Moss green
891	676	▣	30676	Old gold
226	702	⊞	30702	Christmas green
256	704	△	30704	Chartreuse
301	744	▽	30744	Yellow
275	746	⊡	30746	Off-white
1044	895	●	30895	Hunter green
1001	976	◉	30976	Golden brown
306	3820	☒	33820	Straw

BACKSTITCH

360	898	╱	30898	Coffee brown – bow detail and outline, stems, and berry outline (1X)
382	3371	╱	33371	Black-brown – mistletoe leaves and veins, holly leaves (1X)

STRAIGHT STITCH

009	352	╱	30352	Coral – holly berry highlights (1X)
189	991	╱	30991	Aquamarine – spruce branches (2X)

SATIN STITCH

933	543	╱	30543	Beige-brown – mistletoe berries (3X)
046	666	╱	30666	Red – holly berries (3X)

FRENCH KNOT

360	898	●	30898	Coffee brown – berry ends (1X)

MILL HILL BEADS

	○	40557	Gold petite seed beads

Stitch count: *110 high x 180 wide*

Finished design sizes:
25-count fabric – 8⅞ x 14½ inches
28-count fabric – 7⅞ x 12⅞ inches
32-count fabric – 6⅞ x 11¼ inches

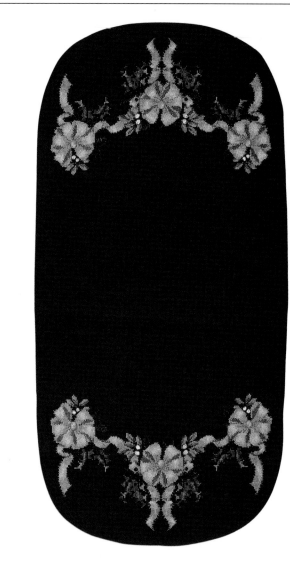

Perfect Rounded Corners

There are several easy ways to make perfectly rounded corners like those on the table runner, *above.*

First, determine the radius of the arc by folding the fabric lengthwise. For a half circle like the one shown, fold the fabric in half. If you prefer a straight span of fabric between the arches, fold the fabric off center. Place the fabric on a pinnable mat or an old magazine.

Measure and mark the distance from the fold to the side edge of the fabric. Measure the same distance from the top along the fold. The point where the two distances meet will be the center of the arc. To mark the arc, use a piece of string and an erasable marker (for smaller projects, use a drawing compass). Tie the string firmly around the barrel of the marker, just above the point. Position the point of the marker on the side edge of the fabric. Holding the marker in that position, pull the thread taut with the opposite end over the marked point on the fabric. Fasten the string to the mat with a thumbtack or straight pin. Move the point of the marker across the fabric to the top of the fabric (see diagram, *right*).

Another method that works for smaller projects is tracing the curve of a dinner plate or larger platter with an erasable marker.

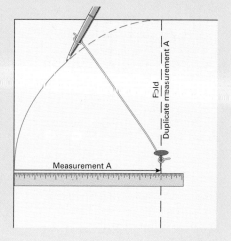

JOY PILLOW
As shown on page 32.

Fabric and Thread
Purchased pillow with a 6¼×12¼"
  insert of 26-count Hickory
  Heatherfield fabric
Cotton embroidery floss in the
  colors listed in the key on *page 44*

Supplies
Needle
6×12" rectangular pillow form

Instructions
Find the center of the chart, *pages 44–45,* and the center of the pillow; begin stitching there. Use three plies of floss to work the cross-stitches over two threads of the fabric. Work the backstitches using one ply of floss. Press the finished stitchery from the back. Insert the pillow form.

SLEDDING-MICE STOCKING AND BOX
As shown on page 33, the finished stocking measures 18" tall and 12" wide; the finished box measures 6¼" in diameter and 3¼" tall.

Fabric and Thread
18×22" piece of 28-count White
  Brittney fabric
Cotton embroidery floss in the
  colors listed in the key on *page 48*
Two spools of Kreinik star blue
  (094) blending filament
Two spools of Kreinik sky blue
  (014) #8 fine braid

Supplies for stocking
Needle
Needlework frame
Erasable fabric marking pen
10-squares-per-inch graph paper
½ yard of polyester fleece
½ yard of red-and-green Christmas
  print fabric
1¼ yards purchased red piping
Red sewing thread
⅜ yard of purchased ¼"-wide red
  flat braid
¼ yard of green rattail cord

Supplies for box
6¼"-diameter round papier mâché
  box with picture frame insert
¼ yard of green-and-white
  print fabric

4¼" circle of polyester fleece
  or batting
¼ yard of green felt
⅝ yard ¼"-wide green-and-
  gold braid
Fabric glue

Instructions
Zigzag or overcast the edges of the Brittney fabric to prevent fraying. With the 22" edge at the top, measure 8" from the right edge of the fabric and 2" from the top; begin stitching the top of the tree indicated by the arrow on the chart, *pages 46–47,* there. Use three plies of floss to work all cross-stitches. Use two plies of floss and one ply of blending filament to work the blended-needle half cross-stitches. Use one ply of floss or braid to work the backstitches. Use the erasable marking pen to draw the outline of the stocking onto the fabric as indicated by the dashed line on the chart. (There will be about 12" of unstitched fabric to the left of the stocking top.)

For the name, use the alphabet, *page 49,* to chart desired name on graph paper, leaving two squares between letters. Find the center of the chart and the vertical center of the unstitched fabric above the foot. Measure 3" from the top. Begin stitching the name there, working cross-stitches with three plies of floss and backstitches with one ply.

For the single mouse, find the center of the chart, *page 48,* and measure 5" below bottom of name and at least 4" from the left edge of the fabric; begin stitching there, working all stitches as directed for stocking. Press the stitched pieces.

To construct the stocking, use ½" seams. Cut out the stocking ½" beyond the edge of the drawn line. Use the stocking as a pattern to cut one interfacing piece from polyester fleece and one back and two lining pieces from Christmas fabric. For the cuff, cut a 19½×15" rectangle from the Christmas fabric, and a 19½×4¼" interfacing rectangle from the fleece. Baste the stocking interfacing to the back of the stitched stocking. Then baste the piping to the front along the drawn line. With right sides together, sew the stitched stocking and back

together, leaving the top open. Clip the curves, turn right side out, and press. Fold the cuff rectangle in half lengthwise with wrong sides together and press. Unfold and position one long edge of the interfacing along the fold and pin. With right sides together, sew the short ends of the cuff together. Trim the excess fleece close to the stitching and press the seam open. Remove any pins and refold the cuff, wrong sides together, along the lengthwise pressed fold, bringing raw edges together. Sew a gathering thread through both layers ½" from raw edges. Pin the cuff to the top of the stocking, using gathering threads to ease cuff to fit stocking.

Stitch the lining pieces together, leaving the top and a 4" space at the bottom of the foot open. *Do not turn.* Slip the stocking and cuff inside the lining. Stitch around the top of the stocking through all layers. Turn the stocking right side out through the opening in the foot of the lining. Sew the opening in the foot closed and push the lining inside the stocking. Fold the cuff along the edge of the interfacing. Press well.

Trim each edge of the stitched name ⅞" beyond stitching, and press the raw edges under ½". Center the name on the cuff and pin. Unfold cuff and topstitch close to the fold through the name, both cuff layers, and the cuff interfacing. Starting at a corner of the name, pin the braid around the edges of the name so it overlaps slightly. Topstitch the braid in the same manner as the name.

Refold the cuff along the edge of the interfacing. For a hanging loop, fold the rattail cord in half and sew the cut ends to the inside of the cuff.

For the box, from green-and-white print, cut a 19½×4" rectangle for box sides, a 19½×1½" rectangle for lid sides, and a 9½"-diameter circle for box top. From the green felt, cut a 19½×3" rectangle for box lining sides and three 6"-diameter circles for the lid lining, the box lining bottom, and the box bottom.

Remove the inner cardboard circle from the lid. Center the fleece on the inner circle and glue. Center the
Continued

lid over the stitched single mouse. Use the erasable marker to trace around the lid on the fabric. Cut out just inside the drawn line. Center the stitched piece over the fleece. Lift the edges of the stitched piece, spread glue on the portion of the cardboard not covered by fleece, and press the fabric into the glue, pulling fabric as taut over fleece as possible. Glue one green felt circle to the other side of the cardboard circle. Set aside.

Fold one short edge of the green-and-white rectangle under ¼". Spread glue on the outer sides of the box. Starting with the unfolded short edge of the rectangle, wrap it around the box, centering it on the sides of the

box with the excess fabric extending above the rim and below the bottom by about ½". Overlap the folded edge to cover the raw edge. Press the fabric to stick and smooth it. Apply glue to the wrong side of fabric at the top rim of the box, fold it to the inside, and press to stick. Apply glue to the fabric at the bottom and press it to the bottom of the box, folding small, evenly spaced tucks into the fabric as you work.

On one long edge of the 19½×3" felt rectangle, make ½"-deep clips at ½" intervals. Apply glue to the back side of the felt and stick it to the inside walls of the box with the unclipped long edge aligned with

the top edge of the box and the clipped edge extending onto the bottom. Apply glue to one of the felt circles and stick it to the inside bottom of the box. Trim ⅛" from the edges of the other circle, apply glue to the back side, and stick it to the bottom of the box.

Center the box lid, rim up, on the wrong side of the green-and-white circle. Use the erasable marker to trace around the inner opening. Cut out ½" inside the drawn line. Clip at ¼" intervals from the cut edge to the drawn line. Apply glue to the wrong side of the fabric and stick it to the lid, folding the clipped edge to the inside. Smooth the fabric at the

JOY PILLOW

Anchor		DMC	
002	⊡	000	White
1006	▣	304	Medium Christmas red
9046	⊠	321	True Christmas red
398	▨	415	Light pearl gray
230	▲	909	Dark emerald
229	◉	910	True emerald
205	▢	911	Medium emerald

BACKSTITCHING

403	╱	310	Black

Stitch count: *54 high x 129 wide*
Finished design sizes:
26-count fabric – 4⅛ x 10 inches
28-count fabric – 3⅞ x 9⅛ inches

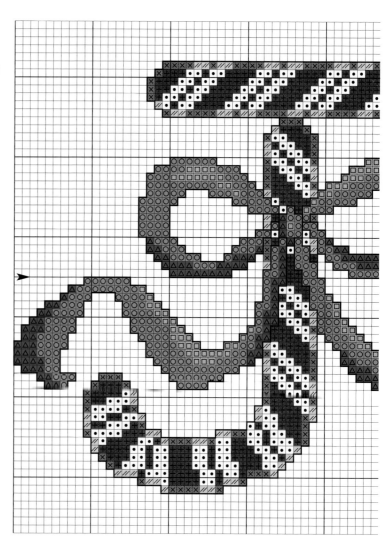

outer edge to the sides of the lid's rim, folding small, evenly spaced tucks into the fabric as you work. Then fold the remaining fabric to the inner sides of the lid's rim.

Fold both the long edges and one short edge of the lid side's rectangle under ¼". Apply glue to the back of the fabric. Starting with the raw-edge end, stick the fabric to the lid's rim, overlapping the folded short edge to cover the raw edge. Center the braid on the rim and glue.

Trim any felt that extends beyond the edge of the cardboard circle. Insert the circle back into the box lid so the stitched piece shows through the opening.

Signing Your Cross-Stitch

After you've finished any Christmas cross-stitch piece, add your name and the date. Decide how much information you want to include— from simple initials and a two-digit year to full names of the giver and recipient, their relationship, source of the pattern, and the full date of presentation. Then use one of these methods.

Chart the letters of your name or your initials and the date on graph paper. Backstitch them into a corner of the piece.

Sign your name and the year in longhand with an air-soluble marker. Stem-stitch the outline with embroidery floss.

Sign with a permanent fabric marker (sold in quilt stores).

Attach a separate label worked on cross-stitch fabric or muslin.

Stem Stitch

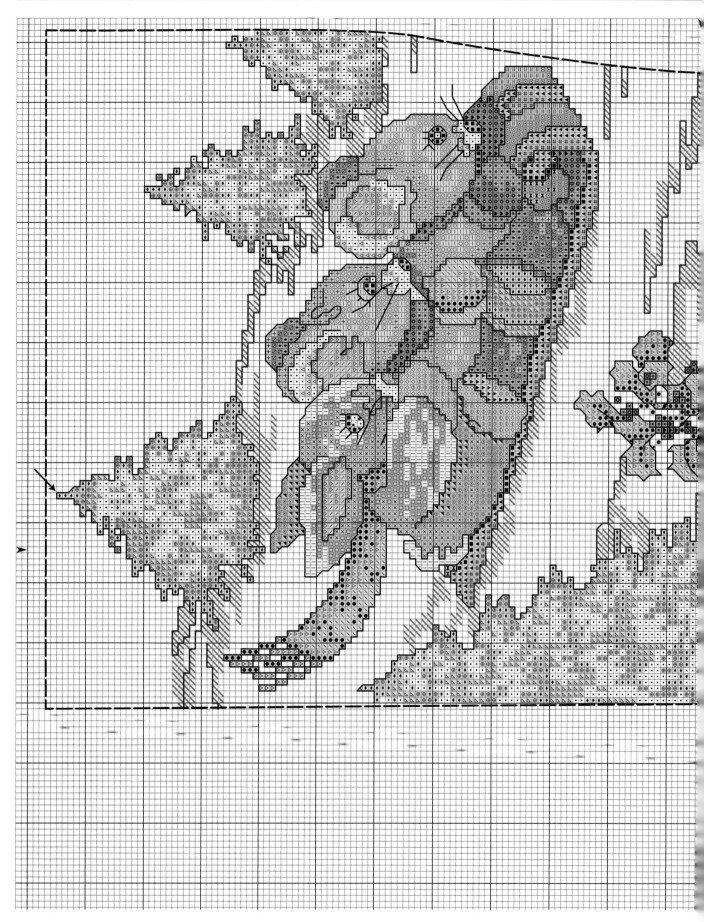

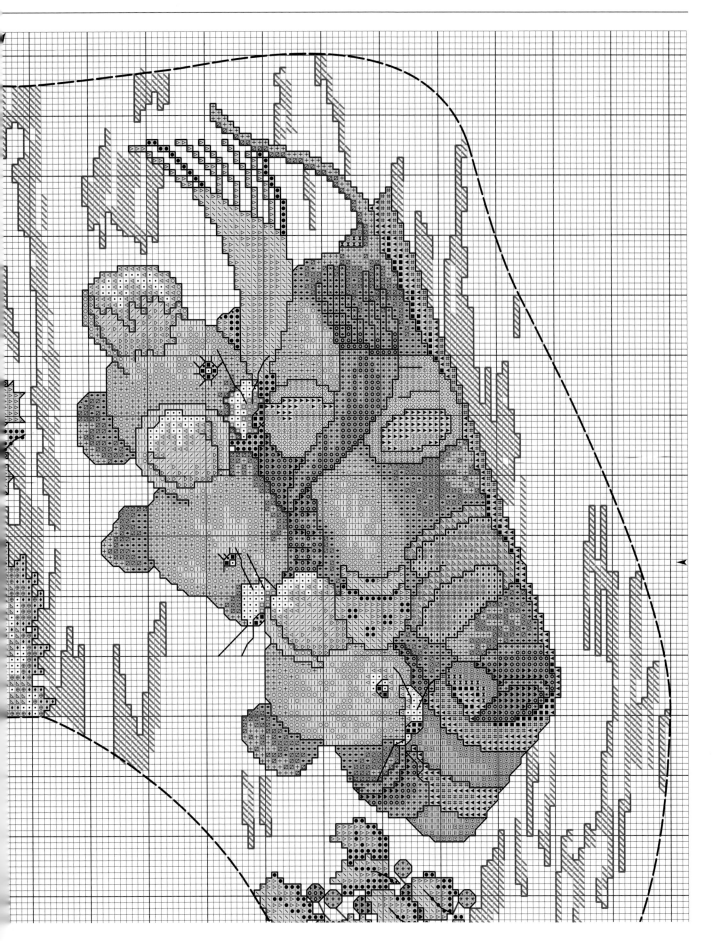

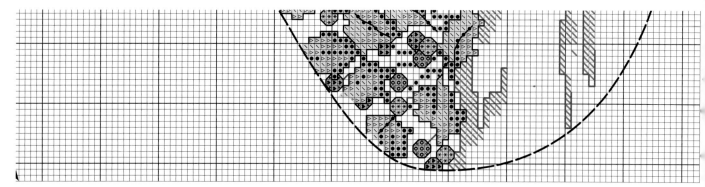

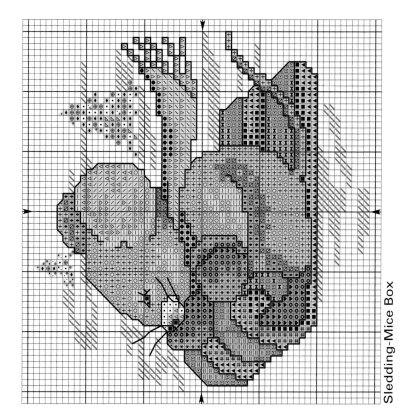

Sledding-Mice Box

Box Stitch count: 58 high x 60 wide
Finished design sizes:
28-count fabric – 4¹/₈ x 4¹/₄ inches
32-count fabric – 3⁵/₈ x 3³/₄ inches
36-count fabric – 3¹/₈ x 3¹/₃ inches

Stocking Stitch count: 231 high x 173 wide
Finished design sizes:
28-count fabric – 16¹/₂ x 12¹/₄ inches
32-count fabric – 14³/₈ x 10³/₄ inches
36-count fabric – 12³/₄ x 9¹/₂ inches

SLEDDING-MICE STOCKING AND BOX

Anchor		DMC	
387			Ecru
002		000	White
893		224	Shell pink
1049		301	Medium mahogany
403		310	Black
013		349	Coral
351		400	Dark mahogany
1047		402	Pale mahogany
401		413	Pewter
235		414	Steel
267		470	Medium avocado
266		471	Light avocado
253		472	Pale avocado
1005		498	Red
212		561	Dark seafoam
210		562	Medium seafoam
208		563	True seafoam
168		597	Medium turquoise
167		598	Light turquoise
234		762	Gray
168		807	Peacock blue
045		814	Garnet
164		824	Deep bright blue
162		825	Dark bright blue
161		826	Medium bright blue
360		839	Dark beige-brown
379		840	Medium beige-brown
378		841	True beige-brown
388		842	Light beige-brown
1003		922	Copper
881		945	Ivory
073		963	Rose-pink

BLENDED-NEEDLE HALF CROSS-STITCH

1037		3756 Baby blue (2X) and
		194 Kreinik Pale blue filament (1X)

BACKSTITCH

403		310 Black – all remaining backstitches
013		349 Coral – berry stems
		014 Kreinik Sky blue #8 braid – snow

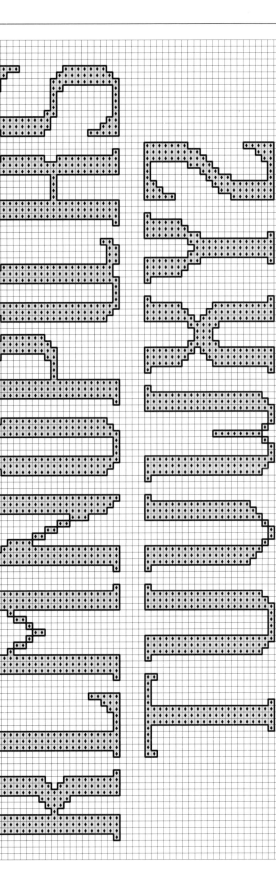

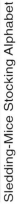

Sledding-Mice Stocking Alphabet

Treasured
TREE TRIMS

Handmade ornaments connect our Christmas experiences—past, present, and future—and make the tree the heart of holiday decor. The beautiful trims in this chapter were designed for years of holiday enjoyment. Start by adding old-fashioned sentiments to packages. These Victorian-style ornaments, right, *stitch up easily on 14-count Aida cloth and finish fast with braid and self-stick mounting board.* Instructions begin on page 58.

Design: Alice Okon

TREASURED TREE TRIMS

For heirloom-to-be ornaments, combine classic style and loving stitches. With her billowy skirt, the timeless Gibson-girl-style angel, opposite, can perch on the tree top or sit on a floral cone—an elegant addition to an angel collection. Not only are the ornaments below exquisite, they're easy to make. Choose a motif and stitch it six times. For an even quicker version, alternate three fabric gores with three cross-stitched ones. Complete instructions begin on page 61.

Designs: Angel, Carol Emmer; Gore balls, Linda Palmer

TREASURED TREE TRIMS

Each of these two delicate needle rolls, right, *requires only one floss color. Add matching beads and an almost effortless ribbon pouf for sparkle. Complete instructions begin on* page 63.

Egg-shaped ornaments in jewel colors with metallic accents, opposite, *brighten any tree, package, or even a pretty bottle. A choice of threads and fabrics allows you to make each of these unique ornaments from the same chart. Complete instructions begin on* page 67.

Designs: Needle rolls, Ursala Michael;
Eggs, Elizabeth Spurlock

Ornaments bring the spirit of Christmas to every nook and cranny of the house. For a bright and airy note, stitch these lighthearted trims, opposite, *on perforated paper (substitute plastic canvas for outdoor use) and add them to a wreath. Each one has an attached cutout that moves in the breeze. Or, grace your home twice with petite stockings,* below. *Stitch them together on pale pink linen to soften an empty wall space. Then, work each one on shiny 11-count damask Aida with glossy rayon thread and finish as tiny gift bags. Complete instructions for both projects begin on* page 68.

Designs: Alice Okon

VICTORIAN ORNAMENTS

As shown on pages 50–51, the finished ornaments are 4¾"-tall.

Fabric and Thread

For each ornament
6×8" piece of 16-count Natural Lite Aida cloth
5×6" piece of lightweight fusible interfacing
3½×4⅝" piece of cream felt
Cotton embroidery floss in the colors listed in the key *below*
DMC metallic gold floss

Supplies
Needle
Needlework frame

3½×4⅝" piece of self-stick mounting board with foam
1 yard of ⅜"-wide red flat trim
Crafts glue

Instructions

Zigzag-stitch or overcast the edges of the fabric to prevent fraying. Find the center of the desired chart and the center of the fabric; begin stitching there. Use two plies of floss to work the cross-stitches. Work the backstitches using one ply of floss unless otherwise specified in the key. Use two plies of floss to work the lazy daisy stitches. Work the French knots using one ply of floss wrapped once around the needle. Press the finished stitchery carefully from the back. Fuse the interfacing to the back of the stitchery, following the manufacturer's instructions.

Peel the protective paper from the mounting board. Center the foam side on the back of the stitchery and press to stick. Trim the fabric ½" beyond the edges of the mounting board. Fold the excess fabric to the back and glue.

Glue the red trim around the front edge of the ornament, overlapping the ends of the trim at the top center of the ornament. Make three 4"-long loops from the remaining red trim. Glue the three-loop hanger to the top center of the ornament. Glue the felt to the back of the ornament.

VICTORIAN ORNAMENTS

Anchor	DMC	
002	000	White
215	320	True pistachio
9046	321	True Christmas red
214	368	Light pistachio
914	407	Medium cocoa
398	415	Light pearl gray
1005	498	Dark Christmas red
936	632	Deep cocoa
891	676	Light old gold
886	677	Pale old gold
890	729	Medium old gold
361	738	Tan
302	743	True yellow
300	745	Light yellow
1012	754	Medium peach
1021	761	Salmon
234	762	Pale pearl gray
144	800	Delft blue
045	814	Dark garnet
1005	816	Light garnet
1011	948	Light peach
298	972	Canary
246	986	Dark forest green
244	987	Medium forest green
242	989	Pale forest green
905	3021	Brown-gray
868	3779	Terra-cotta
035	3801	Watermelon
305	3821	Straw
386	3823	Pale yellow
	282	Metallic gold

BACKSTITCH

Anchor	DMC	
002	000	White – eye highlights
352	300	Mahogany – angel's hair
235	414	Steel – Santa's facial and eye detail, beard, and trim on hat and cuff, angel's wings, globe and lace trim around New Year, and candle
1046	435	Chestnut – candlewick
901	680	Dark old gold – angel's hair, edge of angel ribbon
310	780	Topaz – Santa's banner outline

Anchor	DMC	
307	783	Christmas gold – candle flame and rays
045	814	Dark garnet – angel ribbons, Santa's clothing and mouth, and berries and bows on New Year, and Peace on Earth lettering
1005	816	Light garnet – New Year border
380	838	Beige-brown – holly berries
218	890	Deep pistachio – angel's wreath, Santa's bag, holly leaves, and veins on leaves (2X)
246	986	Dark forest green – New Year lettering
905	3021	Brown-gray – angel's eyes and Santa lettering
059	3350	Dusty rose – angel mouths
1007	3772	Dark cocoa – angel's bodies and face detail
236	3799	Charcoal – angel's eyes, and Santa's pupils
	284	Metallic dark gold – border around Santa

Angel Wreath stitch count: 62 high × 50 wide
Angel Wreath finished design sizes:
16-count fabric – 3⅞ × 3⅛ inches
14-count fabric – 4⅜ × 3½ inches
18-count fabric – 3½ × 2¾ inches

Santa Claus stitch count: 73 high × 54 wide
Santa Claus finished design sizes:
16-count fabric – 4½ × 3⅜ inches
14-count fabric – 5¼ × 3⅞ inches
18-count fabric – 4 × 3 inches

New Year stitch count: 69 high × 49 wide
New Year finished design sizes:
16-count fabric – 4⅜ × 3 inches
14-count fabric – 5 × 3½ inches
18-count fabric – 3⅞ × 2¾ inches

Peace Angel stitch count: 65 high × 52 wide
Peace Angel finished design sizes:
16-count fabric – 4 × 3¼ inches
14-count fabric – 4⅝ × 3¾ inches
18-count fabric – 3⅝ × 2⅞ inches

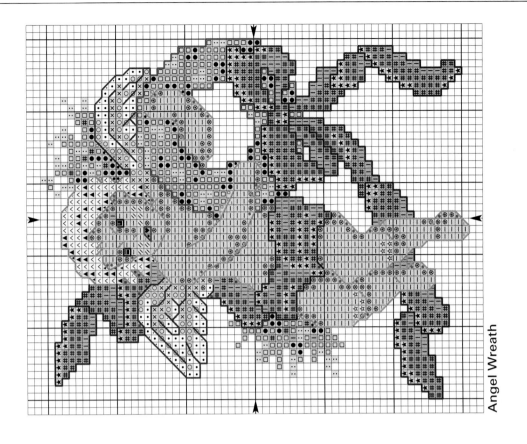

Angel Wreath

New Year

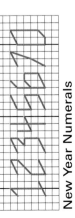

New Year Numerals

TREASURED TREE TRIMS

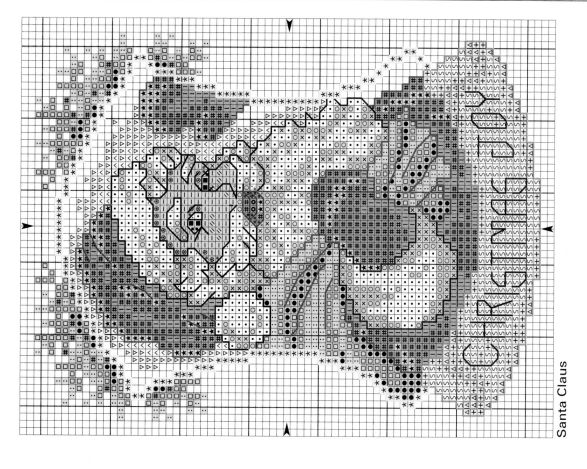

Santa Claus

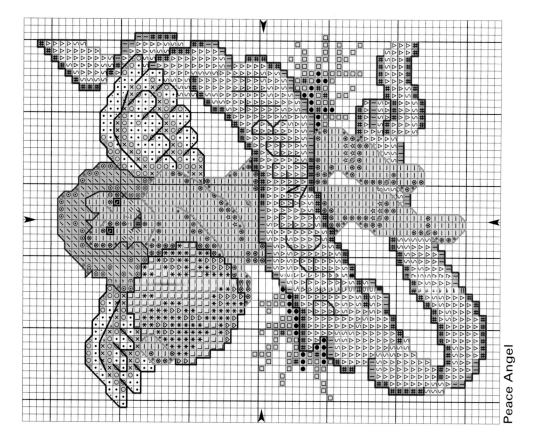

Peace Angel

ANGEL TREE TOPPER

As shown on page 52, the finished tree topper is 16" tall, including the skirt.

Fabric and Thread

12×14" piece of 28-count Raw linen Cashel linen
9×11" piece of fusible interfacing
1 yard of 45"-wide white batiste fabric
Cotton embroidery floss in the colors listed in the key on *page 63*
Kreinik blending filament in the colors listed in the key on *page 63*
Kreinik 002P gold cable

Supplies

Needle
Embroidery hoop
2 packages of Mill Hill 12147 Matte light topaz flower Glass Treasures
Mill Hill 42011 Victorian gold petite seed beads
Air-soluble fabric marker
Matching sewing thread

Instructions

Zigzag-stitch or overcast the edges of the fabric to prevent fraying. Find the center of the chart, *pages 62–63,* and the center of the fabric; begin stitching there. Use two plies of floss to work the cross-stitches over two threads of the fabric. Work the blended-needle stitches as specified in the key. Use one ply of floss to work the backstitches. Work the straight stitches and the blended-needle straight stitches as specified in the key.

Thread a beading needle with one ply of white floss; knot the ends. Bring the needle up at the position indicated on the chart. Slip the flower bead and a petite seed bead onto the needle. Bring the needle back through the flower bead and into the fabric; tie off. Repeat for the remaining bead stitches. Place the finished stitchery facedown on a soft towel and carefully press from the back. Centering the design, fuse the interfacing to wrong side of stitched fabric following the manufacturer's instructions.

From the batiste, cut two 10×44" skirt rectangles and a 1½×14½" skirt band from the batiste. Use the air-soluble marker to draw the outline around the stitched linen angel as indicated by the dashed lines on the chart. Cut out the angel ½" beyond the marked line. Use the stitched fabric as a pattern to cut two lining ovals and two back ovals from the remaining batiste. Measurements include ¼" seam allowances unless otherwise specified.

Make a small clip or notch at the top and bottom centers of both the stitched linen and the batiste lining ovals. Baste the two lining ovals together with the wrong sides facing; set aside.

Pin the back ovals together, right sides together. Referring to Diagram 1, *right,* for guidance, measure 2¼" from the bottom of the paired back ovals. Use the air-soluble marker to draw a straight line across the fabric. Cut along the drawn line through both pieces of batiste and discard the excess fabric. Mark the top and bottom centers of the angel back shapes. With the right sides of the backs together, sew across the straight edge (see Diagram 2). Turn right side out; press. Topstitch across the straight edge. Align the raw curved edges.

Position the back pieces atop the joined lining ovals, matching the top notches; baste through all layers. Baste a skirt placement line on the lining using the straight seam line of the back as a guide (see Diagram 3). Pin the right side of the stitched angel to the batiste layers so the back shapes are sandwiched between the linen and the lining pieces. With the linen on top, sew around the outside curved edge using a ½" seam and leaving an opening at the bottom for turning. Trim the seams, turn the angel right side out, and press. Hand-stitch the opening closed.

For the skirt, sew the short ends of the skirt rectangles together with right sides facing; press the seams open. Turn the bottom edge of the skirt under ¼" and press. Turn it under another ¼", and hand-stitch. Sew the short ends of the skirt band together to make a continuous circle. Zigzag-stitch or overcast one long straight edge of the skirt band.

Sew two gathering threads around the top edge of the skirt, ¼" and ⅜" from the edge. Pull gathers to fit the raw edge of the skirt band (about 14"). Pin the skirt to the skirt band with raw edges even. Adjust the gathers evenly and stitch. Fold the skirt band over the raw edge of the skirt; topstitch through all layers.

Pin the right side of the skirt back to the wrong side of the angel back. Position it far enough inside the angel so that the line of gathers does not show. Topstitch directly on top of previous topstitching. Pin the other side of the skirt along the basting line. Hand-stitch the skirt front to the angel lining.

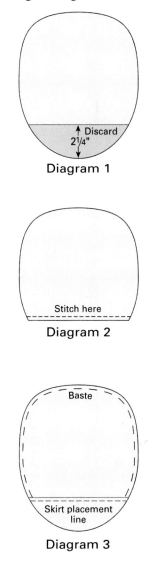

Diagram 1

Discard
2¼"

Diagram 2

Stitch here

Diagram 3

Baste

Skirt placement line

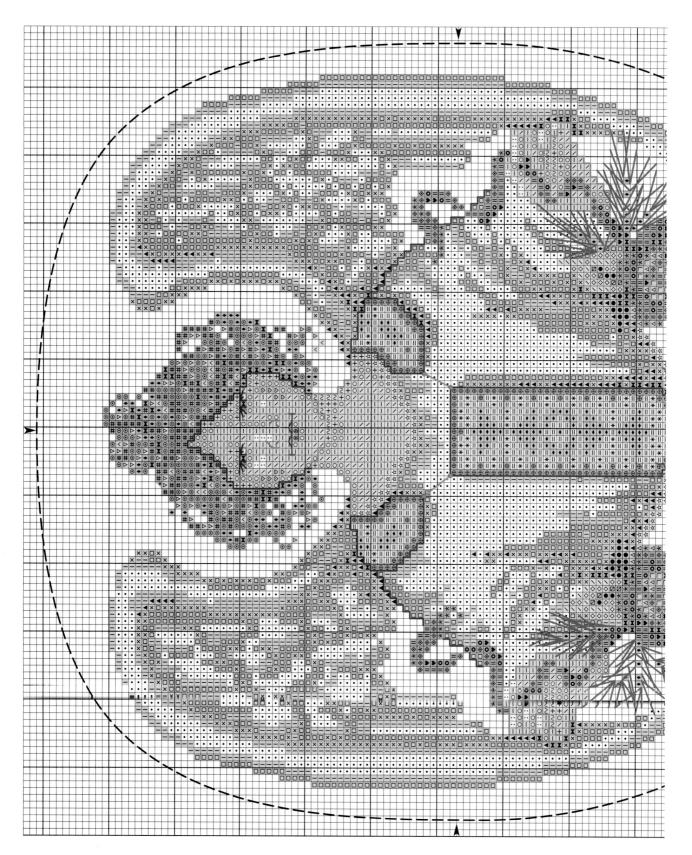

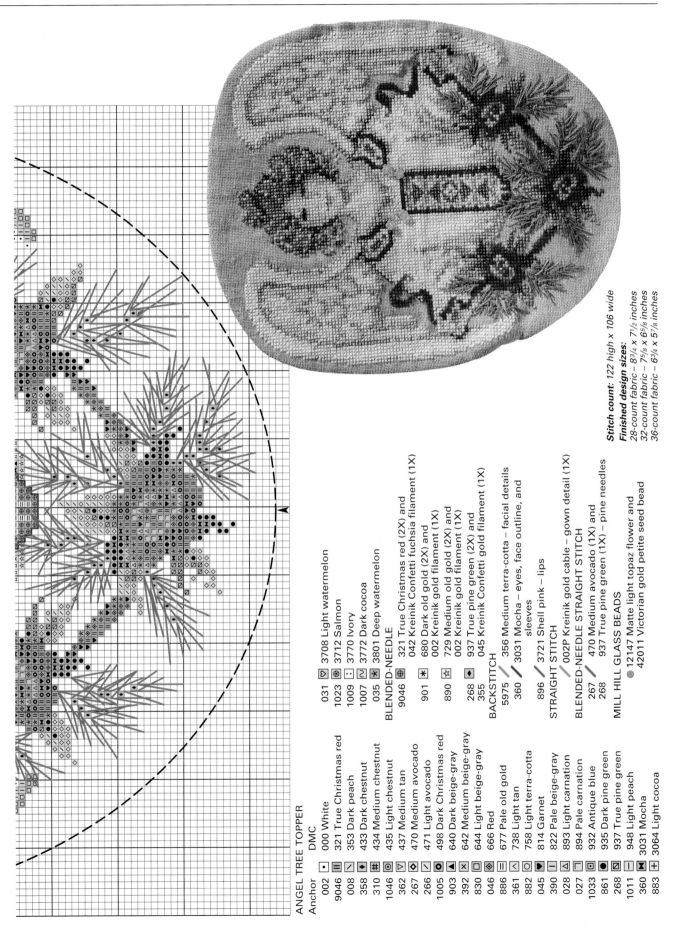

ANGEL TREE TOPPER

Anchor   DMC

002	•	000 White
9046	▪	321 True Christmas red
008	╱	353 Dark peach
358	◆	433 Dark chestnut
310	⊞	434 Medium chestnut
1046	◨	435 Light chestnut
362	▷	437 Medium tan
267	◇	470 Medium avocado
266	◿	471 Light avocado
1005	◉	498 Dark Christmas red
903	◀	640 Dark beige-gray
392	✕	642 Medium beige-gray
830	▢	644 Light beige-gray
046	▣	666 Red
886	⊫	677 Pale old gold
361	◁	738 Light tan
882	◯	758 Light terra-cotta
045	▶	814 Garnet
390	▭	822 Pale beige-gray
028	△	893 Light carnation
027	⬚	894 Pale carnation
1033	◱	932 Antique blue
861	●	935 Dark pine green
268	▨	937 True pine green
1011	▮	948 Light peach
360	✖	3031 Mocha
883	+	3064 Light cocoa

031	▽	3708 Light watermelon
1023	✳	3712 Salmon
1009	⦂	3770 Ivory
1007	◠	3772 Dark cocoa
035	✴	3801 Deep watermelon

BLENDED-NEEDLE

9046	⊕	321 True Christmas red (2X) and
		042 Kreinik Confetti fuchsia filament (1X)
901	✳	680 Dark old gold (2X) and
		002 Kreinik gold filament (1X)
890	☆	729 Medium old gold (2X) and
		002 Kreinik gold filament (1X)
268	◆	937 True pine green (2X) and
355		045 Kreinik Confetti gold filament (1X)

BACKSTITCH

5975	╱	356 Medium terra-cotta – facial details
360	╱	3031 Mocha – eyes, face outline, and
		sleeves
896	╱	3721 Shell pink – lips

STRAIGHT STITCH

	╱	002P Kreinik gold cable – gown detail (1X)

BLENDED-NEEDLE STRAIGHT STITCH

267	╱	470 Medium avocado (1X) and
268	╱	937 True pine green (1X) – pine needles

MILL HILL GLASS BEADS

	●	12147 Matte light topaz flower and
		42011 Victorian gold petite seed bead

Stitch count: *122 high x 106 wide*

Finished design sizes:
28-count fabric – 8³⁄₄ x 7¹⁄₂ inches
32-count fabric – 7⁵⁄₈ x 6⁵⁄₈ inches
36-count fabric – 6³⁄₄ x 5⁷⁄₈ inches

TREASURED TREE TRIMS

SIX-GORE BALLS

Finished balls, as pictured on page 53, are 4" in diameter.

Fabric and Thread

For Ornament #1
7×7½" piece of 32-count China white linen and 7×7½" piece of hunter green moiré faille

For Ornament #2
7×15" piece of 25-count Cream Dublin linen

For Ornament #3
7×7½" piece of 25-count Cream Dublin linen and 7×7½" piece of ivory moiré faille

Cotton embroidery floss in the colors listed in the key, *below*
Kreinik Gold 002 #8 fine braid

Supplies

Tracing paper
White glue
4" foam ball
6" of rattail or twisted cord
1¼ yards of ½" wide French gimp braid
Straight pins

Instructions

These directions are for an ornament with six stitched gores. Any of the charts *below* may be used for an ornament with three stitched gores by cutting three faille gores and alternating them with three stitched gores.

Zigzag-stitch or overcast the edges of the linen to prevent fraying. Divide the linen into 7×2½" rectangles, basting on the dividing lines. For each gore, find the center of the chart and the center of one

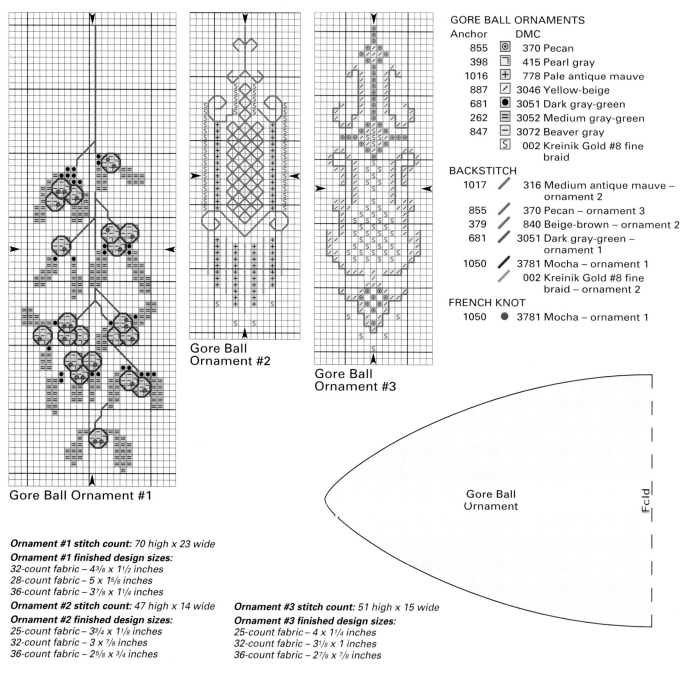

Gore Ball Ornament #1

Gore Ball Ornament #2

Gore Ball Ornament #3

Gore Ball Ornament

GORE BALL ORNAMENTS

Anchor		DMC	
855	⊙	370	Pecan
398	⊓	415	Pearl gray
1016	+	778	Pale antique mauve
887	∕	3046	Yellow-beige
681	●	3051	Dark gray-green
262	≡	3052	Medium gray-green
847	⊟	3072	Beaver gray
	S	002	Kreinik Gold #8 fine braid

BACKSTITCH

1017	∕	316	Medium antique mauve – ornament 2
855	∕	370	Pecan – ornament 3
379	∕	840	Beige-brown – ornament 2
681	∕	3051	Dark gray-green – ornament 1
1050	∕	3781	Mocha – ornament 1
		002	Kreinik Gold #8 fine braid – ornament 2

FRENCH KNOT

| 1050 | ● | 3781 | Mocha – ornament 1 |

Ornament #1 stitch count: *70 high x 23 wide*
Ornament #1 finished design sizes:
32-count fabric – 4³⁄₈ x 1½ inches
28-count fabric – 5 x 1⁵⁄₈ inches
36-count fabric – 3⁷⁄₈ x 1¼ inches

Ornament #2 stitch count: *47 high x 14 wide*
Ornament #2 finished design sizes:
25-count fabric – 3¾ x 1¹⁄₈ inches
32-count fabric – 3 x ⁷⁄₈ inches
36-count fabric – 2⁵⁄₈ x ¾ inches

Ornament #3 stitch count: *51 high x 15 wide*
Ornament #3 finished design sizes:
25-count fabric – 4 x 1¼ inches
32-count fabric – 3¹⁄₈ x 1 inch
36-count fabric – 2⁷⁄₈ x ⁷⁄₈ inches

rectangle. Use two plies of floss or one strand of fine braid to work cross-stitches over two threads of fabric. Use one ply of floss or one strand of fine braid to work back-stitches. When all the gores are stitched, press the fabric carefully from the back.

Fold a piece of tracing paper 5×2" or larger in half lengthwise and trace the gore pattern, *opposite*; cut out and unfold. Center the pattern over the stitching on each rectangle and trace around it. Carefully cut along the drawn lines. (For an ornament with three stitched gores, trace and cut three gores from faille.) Apply a thin line of glue along each raw edge; allow to dry.

Pin one gore to the foam ball with straight pins placed just inside the glue lines. Overlap the long edge of the second gore ⅛" and secure with pins. Continue working around the ball until all six gores have been pinned in place.

Secure one end of the French gimp braid at the top of the ornament with a straight pin. Wrap the braid halfway around the ball, covering the raw edge where two gores overlap. Fasten at the bottom with another pin. Wrap braid back to the starting point, covering the overlap on the opposite side. Secure at the top with another pin. Turn the braid slightly and wrap around the ball again, securing with a pin at the bottom, and covering the next pair of over-laps. Wrap the braid around once more to cover the final pair of over-laps. Insert additional pins to hold the braid in position on the sides of the ornament.

For the hanger, fold the cord in half and knot the ends together. Push a straight pin through the knot and into the ball at the top.

JEWEL-TONE EGGS
As shown on page 54, the finished eggs are 3" tall.

Fabric and Thread
For each ornament
6×6" piece of 18-count Ivory (blue egg), Silver-and-white green egg), or Gold-and-white (red egg) Aida cloth
4×4" piece of fusible interfacing

4×4" piece of felt to match the desired egg
Cotton embroidery floss and/or Needle Necessities overdyed floss in the colors listed in the key on *page 66*
Gold or silver metallic embroidery thread as listed in the key on *page 66*

Supplies
Needle
Embroidery hoop
Medium oval charm kit
For the blue egg
¼ yard of ¼"-diameter gold-and-white twisted cord
Beading needle
12—⅛"-diameter metallic gold beads
Mill Hill 70020 Royal blue small bugle beads
2"-long metallic gold tassel
1 yard of royal blue rattail cord
For the green egg
¼ yard of ⅛"-diameter metallic silver twisted cord
6" length of metallic silver cord
⅝"-diameter silver star button
¾ yard of ⅛"-wide green satin ribbon
4—⅛"-diameter metallic silver beads
For the red egg
¼ yard of ⅛"-diameter red-and-gold cord
25" length of ⅛"-diameter metallic gold cord

Instructions
Zigzag-stitch or overcast the edges of the fabric to prevent fraying. Find the center of the chart, *page 66,* and the center of the fabric; begin stitch-ing there. Use two plies of floss to work the cross-stitches. (When stitching with the overdyed floss, work each stitch completely before proceeding to the next stitch.) Work the backstitches using one ply of floss or one strand of metallic thread. Work the French knots using one ply of floss or one strand metal-lic thread wrapped twice around the needle. Place the finished stitchery facedown on a soft towel and press from the back. Center and fuse the interfacing on the back, following the manufacturer's instructions.

Use the charm back as a pattern to cut a back from the felt. Set the

felt oval aside. Assemble the egg following the instructions on the charm kit.

For the blue egg, dab glue on the ends of the twisted cord and the rat-tail cord to prevent fraying. Beginning at the top center of the oval, glue the twisted cord around the edge of the charm. Thread a beading needle with a doubled length of thread. Anchor the thread at the top center of the ornament. Slip a gold bead, then three blue bugle beads onto the needle. Continue adding beads, alternating one gold with three bugle beads, until there are enough to fit the perimeter inside the cording. Return the thread into the fabric and tie off. Tack or glue the bead string inside the cording. Thread the rattail cord through the loop at the top of the egg. Knot the cord ends. Glue the tassel to the bottom of the oval and the felt oval to the back of the fin-ished charm.

For the green egg, dab glue on the ends of the metallic cords and rib-bon to prevent fraying. Beginning at the top center of the oval, glue the twisted cord around the edge of the charm. Cut two 6" lengths of satin ribbon. Combine the ribbon lengths with the 6" piece of metallic cord. Tack the centers of the combined lengths to the top center of the oval. Sew the star button to the top of the oval. Slip a silver bead onto each end of the satin ribbon. Knot the rib-bon and cord ends. Thread the remaining satin ribbon through the loop at the top of the oval. Glue the felt oval to the back of the charm.

For the red egg, dab glue on the ends of each piece of cord to prevent fraying. Beginning at the top center, glue the red-and-gold cord around the edge of the charm. Thread the metallic gold cord through the loop at the top of the egg. Knot the cord ends. Glue the felt oval to the back of the finished charm.

Jewel-Tone Eggs

JEWEL-TONE EGGS
BLUE EGG

Anchor		DMC
133	☒	796 Royal blue (2X)

BACKSTITCH

	╱	284 DMC Gold metallic embroidery thread (2X)

FRENCH KNOT

| 133 | ● | 796 Royal blue |
| | ● | 284 DMC Gold metallic embroidery thread |

GREEN EGG

Anchor		DMC
923	☒	3818 Emerald (2X)

BACKSTITCH

| 923 | ╱ | 3818 Emerald (1X) |
| | ╱ | 283 DMC Silver metallic embroidery thread – snowflakes (1X) |

FRENCH KNOT

| 923 | ⋮ | 3818 Emerald |

RED EGG

| | ☒ | 152 Needle Necessities Moulin Rouge (2X) |

BACKSTITCH

| 013 | ╱ | 349 Coral (1X) |

FRENCH KNOT

| 013 | ⋮ | 349 Coral |

Stitch count: *50 high x 38 wide*
Finished design sizes:
28-count fabric – 8³/₄ x 7¹/₂ inches
32-count fabric – 7⁵/₈ x 6⁵/₈ inches
36-count fabric – 6³/₄ x 5⁷/₈ inches

HOLIDAY NEEDLE ROLLS

As shown on page 54, finished rolls measure 8×2".

Fabric and Thread
8×16" piece of 28-count white linen
Rayon embroidery floss in the colors listed in the key, *opposite*

Supplies
Needle
Needlework frame
Mill Hill beads in the colors listed in the keys
White, red, and green sewing thread
1 yard each of red and green 3"-wide organza ribbon
Polyester fiberfill
Potpourri (optional)

Instructions
Zigzag-stitch or overcast the edges of the fabric to prevent fraying. Use basting thread to divide the linen into two 8" squares. For each needle roll, measure 1½" from each edge of the top right corner of one square; begin stitching the top row of the chart there. Use three plies of floss for the cross-stitches. Use one ply of floss to work backstitches. Attach the beads as you stitch each row. Place the finished stitchery right side down on a terry cloth towel and press carefully from the back.

For each roll, trim the excess fabric 1¼" above the top row of stitches and 1¼" below the bottom row. Trim each side ½" beyond the stitching. Press the top and bottom edges under ½"; unfold. Press

one side under ½" and position the fold at the edge of the stitching on the other side, aligning the rows. Slip-stitch together. Refold the top and bottom edge under. Run a gathering thread close to the bottom fold. Pull to close the bottom edge and secure the thread. Stuff firmly with fiberfill, adding potpourri in the middle, if desired. Run another gathering thread close to the top fold. Pull to close and secure the thread.

For the puffs on the ends, cut the corresponding colored ribbon into two 18" lengths. Run a gathering thread lengthwise down the center of each piece. Pull the gathering thread as tightly as possible and secure it, but do not cut. Use the remaining thread to stitch the puff to one end of the needle roll.

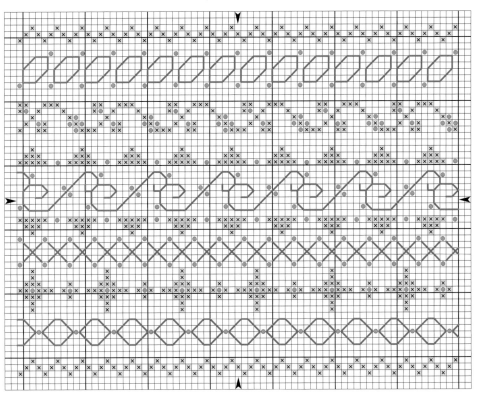

Green Needle Roll

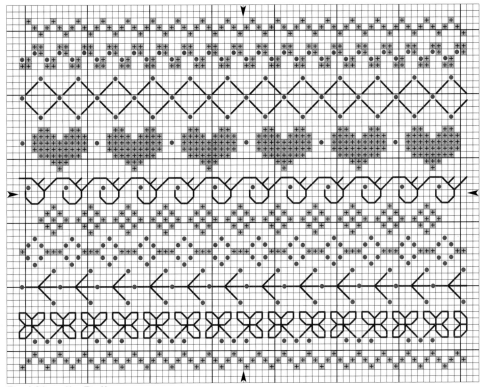

Red Needle Roll

Stitch count: *72 high x 55 wide*
Finished design sizes:
28-count fabric – 5¹/₈ x 4 inches
32-count fabric – 4¹/₂ x 3¹/₂ inches
36-count fabric – 4 x 3 inches

HOLIDAY NEEDLE ROLLS

Marlitt		DMC Rayon Floss
1017	⊞	30666 Red
811	☒	30700 Green

Marlitt		DMC Rayon Floss
BACKSTITCH		
1017	╱	30666 Red – red ornament
811	╱	30700 Green – green ornament

MILL HILL GLASS BEADS
● 00165 Christmas red – red ornament
● 00167 Christmas green – green ornament

LIGHTHEARTED ORNAMENTS
As shown on page 56.

Fabric and Thread
For each ornament
6×8" piece of 14-count white perforated paper
3½×4⅝" piece of cream felt
Cotton embroidery floss in the colors listed in the key *below*
DMC metallic gold floss
Kreinik 002 Gold #8 braid

Supplies
Needle
Crafts glue

Instructions

Find the center of the desired chart and the center of the perforated paper; begin stitching there. Use two plies of floss to work the cross-stitches. Work the backstitches using one ply of floss unless otherwise specified in the key. Use two plies of floss to work the lazy daisy stitches. Work the French knots using one ply of floss wrapped once around the needle.

Cut out the shapes one square beyond the outer stitches of the design. Use the perforated paper shapes as patterns to cut matching backs from the felt. Set the felt pieces aside. Referring to the photograph on *page 56* for guidance, glue four plies of Christmas red floss (DMC 321) between the appropriate pieces for each ornament. For the hanger, fold a 7" length of gold floss in half and glue the ends to the top of the ornament. Glue the felt to the back of the ornament.

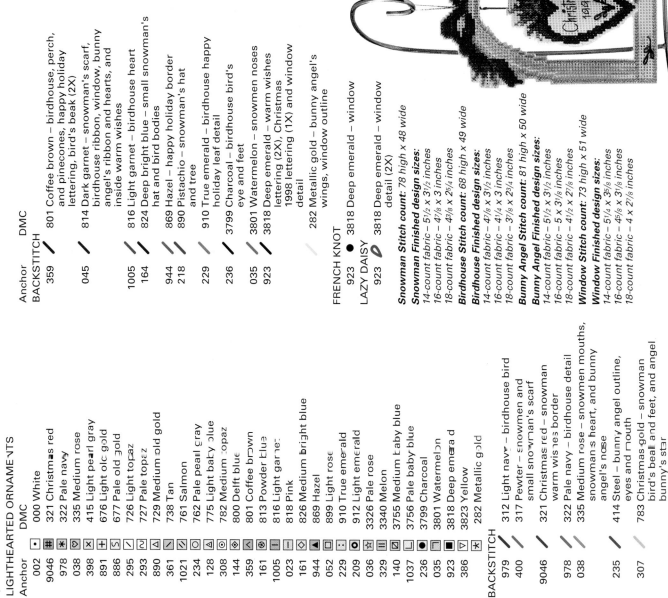

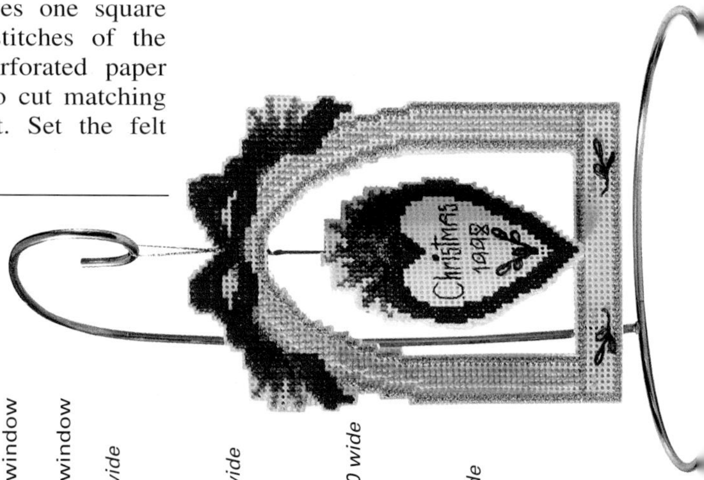

LIGHTHEARTED ORNAMENTS

Symbol	Anchor	DMC	Color
•	002	000	White
#	9046	321	Christmas red
✳	978	322	Pale navy
▷	038	335	Medium rose
✕	398	415	Light pearl gray
+	891	676	Light old gold
∠	886	677	Pale old gold
⌐	295	726	Light topaz
2	293	727	Pale topaz
△	890	729	Medium old gold
╱	361	738	Tan
◁	1021	761	Salmon
◇	234	762	Pale pearl gray
△	128	775	Light baby blue
◆	308	782	Medium topaz
◈	144	800	Delft blue
◁	359	801	Coffee brown
⊕	161	813	Powder blue
–	1005	816	Light garnet
◯	023	818	Pink
◁	161	826	Medium bright blue
∷	944	869	Hazel
○	052	899	Light rose
✳	229	910	True emerald
▣	209	912	Light emerald
⊔	036	3326	Pale rose
=	329	3340	Melon
⌐	140	3755	Medium baby blue
●	1037	3756	Pale baby blue
◨	236	3799	Charcoal
■	035	3801	Watermelon
▷	923	3818	Deep emerald
▷	386	3823	Yellow
✕	282		Metallic gold

BACKSTITCH

Anchor	DMC	Color/use
979	312	Light navy – birdhouse bird
400	317	Pewter – snowmen and small snowman's scarf
9046	321	Christmas red – snowman warm wishes border
978	322	Pale navy – birdhouse detail
038	335	Medium rose – snowmen mouths, snowman's heart, and bunny angel's nose
235	414	Steel – bunny angel outline, eyes and mouth
307	783	Christmas gold – snowman bird's beak and feet, and angel bunny's star
176	793	Cornflower blue – bunny angel's dress
359	801	Coffee brown – birdhouse, perch, and pinecones, happy holiday lettering, bird's beak (2X)
045	814	Dark garnet – snowman's scarf, birdhouse ribbon, window, bunny angel's ribbon and hearts, and inside warm wishes
1005	816	Light garnet – birdhouse heart
164	824	Deep bright blue – small snowman's hat and bird bodies
944	869	Hazel – happy holiday border
218	890	Pistachio – snowman's hat and tree
229	910	True emerald – birdhouse happy holiday leaf detail
236	3799	Charcoal – birdhouse bird's eye and feet
035	3801	Watermelon – snowmen noses
923	3818	Deep emerald – warm wishes lettering (2X), Christmas 1998 lettering (1X) and window detail
282		Metallic gold – bunny angel's wings, window outline

FRENCH KNOT

Anchor	DMC	Color/use
923	3818	Deep emerald – window

LAZY DAISY

Anchor	DMC	Color/use
923	3818	Deep emerald – window detail (2X)

Snowman Stitch count: 78 high x 48 wide
Snowman Finished design sizes:
14-count fabric – 5½ x 3½ inches
16-count fabric – 4⅞ x 3 inches
18-count fabric – 4⅜ x 2¾ inches

Birdhouse Stitch count: 68 high x 49 wide
Birdhouse Finished design sizes:
14-count fabric – 4⅞ x 3½ inches
16-count fabric – 4¼ x 3 inches
18-count fabric – 3⅞ x 2¾ inches

Bunny Angel Stitch count: 81 high x 50 wide
Bunny Angel Finished design sizes:
14-count fabric – 5½ x 3½ inches
16-count fabric – 5 x 3⅛ inches
18-count fabric – 4½ x 2⅞ inches

Window Stitch count: 73 high x 51 wide
Window Finished design sizes:
14-count fabric – 5¼ x 3⅝ inches
16-count fabric – 4⅝ x 3⅛ inches
18-count fabric – 4 x 2⅞ inches

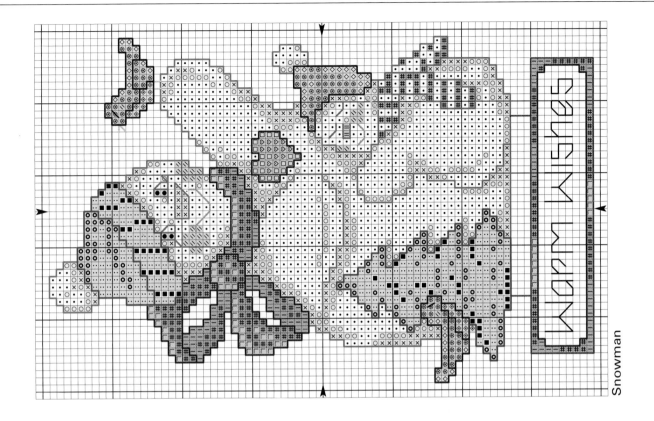

Snowman

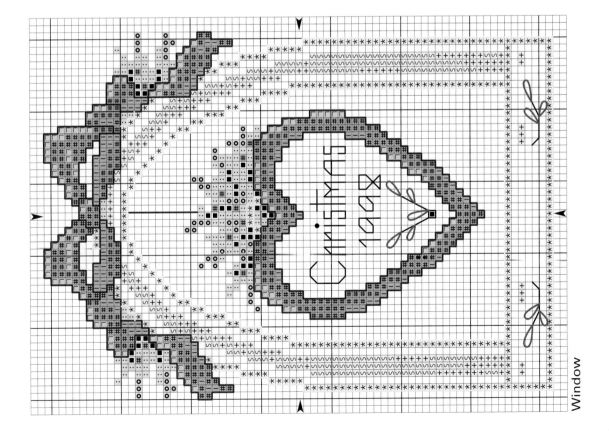

Window

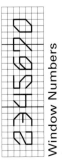

Window Numbers

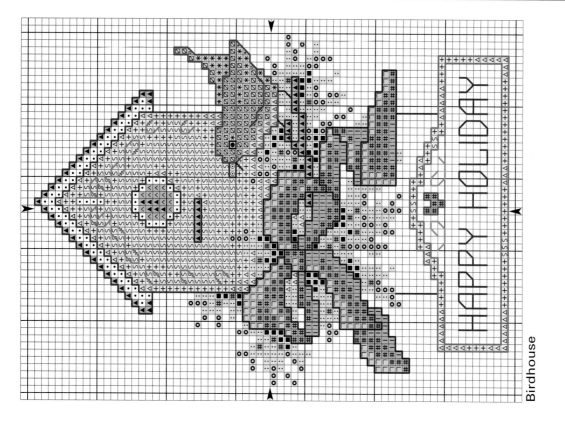

Birdhouse

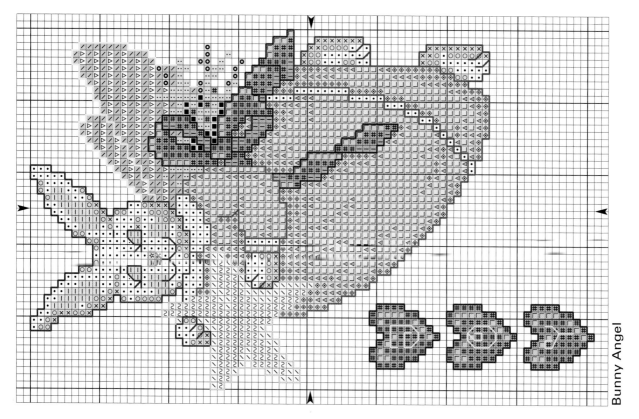

Bunny Angel

TEA ROSE FRAMED STOCKINGS

As shown on page 57.

Fabric and Thread

12×16" piece of 32-count Cherub pink linen

Cotton embroidery floss in the colors listed in the key on *page 72*

Kreinik 002 Gold #8 braid

Supplies

Needle

Needlework frame

Desired frame

Instructions

Zigzag-stitch or overcast the edges of the fabric to prevent fraying. Measure 3½" from the edges on the top corner of the fabric. Begin working the left stitch of the top row of the chart, *pages 72–73,* there. Use two plies of floss or one strand of braid to work the cross-stitches over two threads of the fabric. Work the running-stitch outline using one ply of floss. Work the backstitches using one ply of floss.

Press the finished stitchery from the back. Frame the piece as desired.

TEA ROSE MINI STOCKINGS

As shown on page 57.

Fabric and Thread

For each stocking

6×10" piece of 11-count Ivory Damask Aida cloth

⅜ yard of 45"-wide pink satin fabric

5×9" piece of lightweight fusible interfacing

Rayon embroidery floss in the colors listed in the key on *page 72*

Kreinik 002 Gold #8 braid

Supplies

Needle

Needlework frame

Sewing thread

⅔ yard of ⅛"-diameter piping cord

Instructions

Zigzag-stitch or overcast the edges of the fabric to prevent fraying. Find the center of the desired stocking chart, *pages 72–73,* and the center of the fabric; begin stitching there. Use three plies of floss or one strand of braid to work the cross-stitches. Work the backstitches using two plies of floss. Use a single strand of sewing thread to work the running-stitch outline.

Fuse the interfacing to the back of the stitched fabric, following the manufacturer's instructions. Cut out the fabric ½" beyond the running stitches. Use the stitched stocking as a pattern to cut a matching back from the satin fabric. Also cut a 1½×24" piping strip from the satin.

To make the piping, center the cording lengthwise on the wrong side of the piping strip. Fold the fabric around the cording with the raw edges together. Use a zipper foot to sew through both layers close to the cording. Cut an 18" length of piping and baste it to the sides and bottom of the stocking front with the raw edges even, matching the piping stitching to the running stitches.

With right sides together, pin the stocking front to the back along one side and the bottom only; stitch. Baste the remaining 6" length of covered piping to the top straight edge of the stocking with right sides together and raw edges even; stitch. Finish pinning and then stitching the stocking front to the back around the remaining edge. Trim the seams and clip the curves. Turn the stocking right side out and press lightly. Tack the bottom edge of the top piping to the inside of the stocking.

Working with Rayon Floss

Rayon embroidery floss has a distinctive sheen that makes anything you stitch festive. Because it also is more slippery than cotton floss, it can be difficult to stitch with. Here are some tricks to stitching with it.

Work with slightly shorter lengths of thread (12" instead of the 18" recommended for cotton embroidery floss).

When you work with an even number of plies, start your work with a loop knot (see To secure thread at the beginning, *page 124*). For an odd number of plies, use a waste knot. Make both starting and ending tails extra secure by weaving them under eight to ten stitches.

Some stitchers like to lightly moisten the thread as they stitch. Be sure to test for colorfastness first. Remove the paper bands and rinse the floss in cold water. Lay it on a white paper towel to dry. No color should show on the towel. Don't forget to replace the paper band with the color number on each skein.

Press each stitch between your thumb and forefinger as you work. Rayon creases more easily than cotton, so you'll be putting a bend in the thread that helps it lie smoothly on the fabric.

Converting a chart from cotton to rayon floss adds elegance—and it's fun! As a general rule, you can use the same number of plies. If in doubt, work a test in the corner of your fabric and decide whether you like the coverage.

Be prepared to substitute slightly different shades of colors because rayon floss has a smaller color selection than cotton floss of the same brand. One brand (DMC) uses a direct numbering system for colors (black cotton floss is 310, black rayon is 30310). For the others, you'll have to make your own conversion.

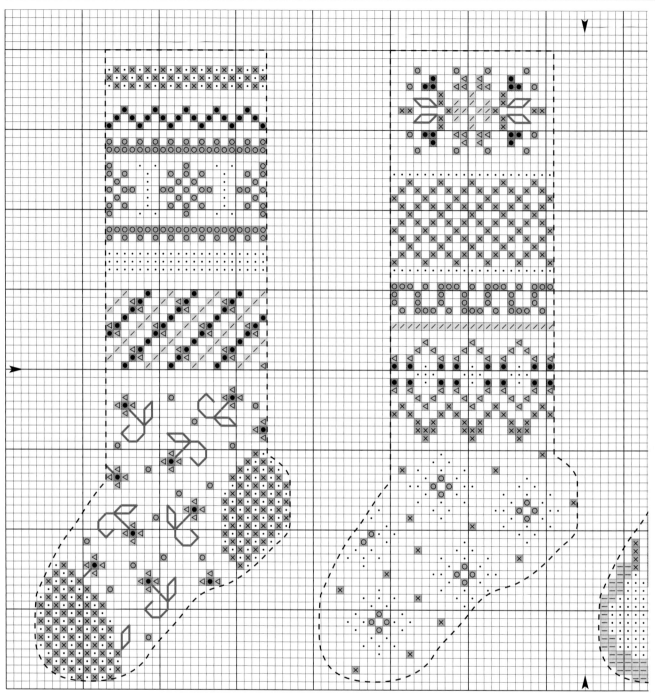

TEA ROSE STOCKINGS

Anchor		DMC Cotton	DMC Rayon	
002	·	000	35200	White
877	/	502	30501	Medium blue-green
875	×	503	30503	True blue-green
234	–	762	30410	Pearl gray
068	◼	3687	33350	True mauve
060	●	3688	30603	Medium mauve
049	◁	3689	33689	Light mauve
	○		002 Kreinik gold #8 braid	

BACKSTITCH

875	/	503	30503	True blue-green

RUNNING STITCH

878	/	501		Dark blue-green

Framed Stockings
Stitch count: *79 high x 144 wide*
Finished design sizes:
22-count fabric – 5 x 9 inches
28-count fabric – 5⅝ x 10¼ inches
36-count fabric – 4⅓ x 8 inches

Mini Stocking
Stitch count: *79 high x 13 wide*
Finished design sizes:
11-count fabric – 7⅛ x 1⅛ inches
14-count fabric – 5⅝ x 1 inches
18-count fabric – 4⅓ x ¾ inches

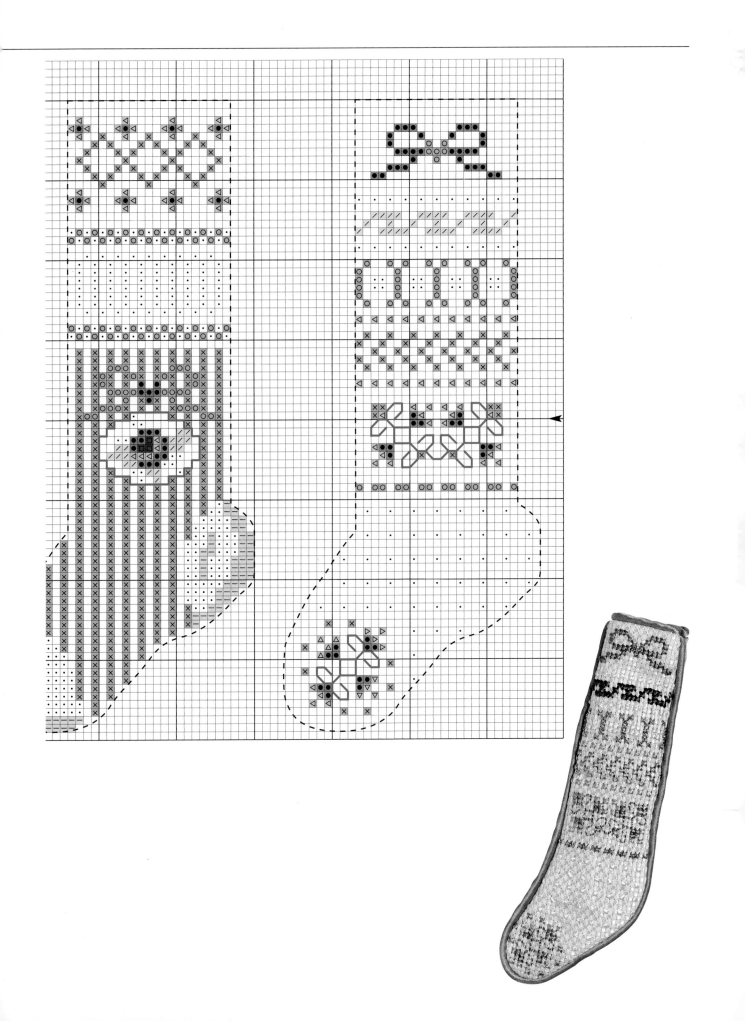

DRESSED
for the
HOLIDAYS

As the song says, Christmas is the time to, "Don our gay apparel." Stitch any or all of these winter wearables and be ready to celebrate the season. The playful snowmen on the front panels of these mother-and-daughter jumpers are certainly enjoying yuletide pleasures. Each jumper comes ready-made with either an Aida or evenweave stitching insert, so there's no finishing to do. Complete instructions are on pages 80–81.

Designs: Jeff Julseth

Winter bird motifs make holiday wearables extra festive. The duplicate-stitch sweater, opposite, *features graceful doves applying golden garland to a tree as an angora-bearded Santa supervises. Cheerful chickadees perched on holly branches adorn a purchased patchwork vest,* above. *Complete instructions for both projects begin on* page 82.

Designs: De Selby

Light up your wardrobe with a quick-to-stitch string of lights, **left.** Stitch the design on a blouse that's made with an evenweave inset, as pictured, or follow our easy instructions to add a simple placket to your own blouse. Instructions begin on page 85.

'Tis the season when Christmas cooks make magic in the kitchen. Here's the cross-stitch recipe for the jolly holiday apron, **opposite:** Combine a snowman, wreath, Santa, and Christmas tree on Aida banding. Add them to a holiday-colored tea towel. Garnish with grosgrain ribbon and bright-hued buttons. Makes every serving stylish. Instructions begin on page 85.

Designs: Blouse, Duffy Morrison; Apron, Helen Nicholson

SNOWMAN JUMPERS
As shown on pages 74–75.

Fabric and Thread
Purchased adult jumper with a 4¼×16" 14-count Aida or 28-count evenweave insert and child's jumper with 2⅝×10½" Aida or evenweave insert

Supplies
Needle

Instructions
Find the center of the insert and the center of the chart; begin stitching there. Use three plies of floss to work the cross-stitches over two threads of the fabric. Work the back-stitches using one ply of floss. Work the blended-needle backstitches as specified in the key. Press the finished stitchery carefully from the back.

Cotton embroidery floss in the colors listed in the keys *opposite*

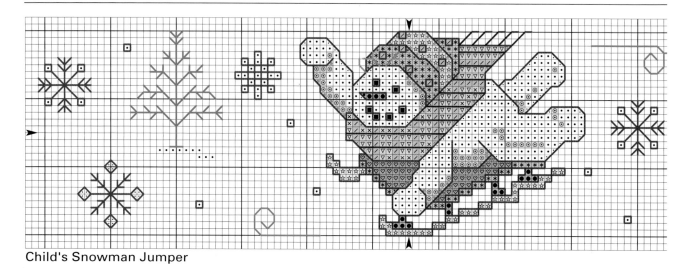

Child's Snowman Jumper

Mother's Snowman Jumper

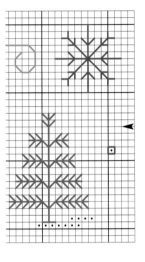

CHILD'S SNOWMAN JUMPER

Anchor		DMC
002	⋅	000 White
342	∕	211 Lavender
042	✳	309 Rose
403	■	310 Black
305	☆	725 True topaz
316	●	740 Tangerine
1005	♡	816 Garnet
229	✕	910 True emerald
209	▽	912 Light emerald
928	◉	3761 Sky blue

BACKSTITCH

002	∕	000 White – snowflakes
212	∕	561 Seafoam – tree on left
309	∕	781 Dark topaz – hair
1005	∕	816 Garnet – scarf and fringe
268	∕	3345 Hunter green – tree on right
381	∕	938 Coffee brown – all remaining backstitches

Anchor		DMC

BLENDED-NEEDLE BACKSTITCH

002	∕	000 White (1X) and
928		3761 Sky blue (1X) – snow swirls

Stitch count: 30 high x 113 wide

Finished design sizes:
30-count fabric – 2 x 7½ inches
28-count fabric – 2⅛ x 8 inches
36-count fabric – 1⅝ x 6¼ inches

MOTHER'S SNOWMAN JUMPER

Anchor		DMC
002	⋅	000 White
342	∕	211 Lavender
042	✳	309 Rose
403	■	310 Black
305	☆	725 True topaz
316	●	740 Tangerine
1005	♡	816 Garnet
229	✕	910 True emerald
209	▽	912 Light emerald
928	◉	3761 Sky blue

BACKSTITCH

002	∕	000 White – snowflakes
212	∕	561 Seafoam – tree on left
309	∕	781 Dark topaz – hair
1005	∕	816 Garnet – scarf and fringe
268	∕	3345 Hunter green – tree on right
381	∕	938 Coffee brown – all remaining backstitches

BLENDED-NEEDLE BACKSTITCH

002	∕	000 White (1X) and
928		3761 Sky blue (1X) – snow swirls

Stitch count: 52 high x 155 wide

Finished design sizes:
28-count fabric – 3¾ x 11 inches
30-count fabric – 3½ x 10⅓ inches
36-count fabric – 2⅞ x 8⅝ inches

DRESSED FOR THE HOLIDAYS

SAVED BY THE BIRDS DUPLICATE-STITCH SWEATER

As shown on page 76.

Fabric and Thread
Purchased navy cotton
  stockinette-stitch crew-neck
  sweater with a gauge of 7 stitches
  and 10 rows = 1 inch
Cotton embroidery floss in the
  colors listed in the key *opposite*
Kreinik 002 Gold 1/16" ribbon
Angora yarn

Supplies
Measuring tape
Tapestry needle

Instructions
Find the vertical center of the sweater front; sew a line of basting stitches from the top to the bottom of the sweater. Mark a point 1" below the lower edge of the neck-band along the basting; begin stitching the top stitch of the star there.

Use six plies of floss, one strand of ribbon, or one strand of angora yarn to work the duplicate stitches (see diagram, *opposite*). Work the French-knot Santa's eye using six plies of floss wrapped once around the needle. Work the French-knot ornaments using 12 plies of floss wrapped once around the needle.

For each sleeve, find the center of the bottom row of the sleeve chart; find the center of the sleeve and measure 5½" from the top of the ribbing; begin stitching there. Repeat the motif as necessary around the sleeve. Remove the basting thread.

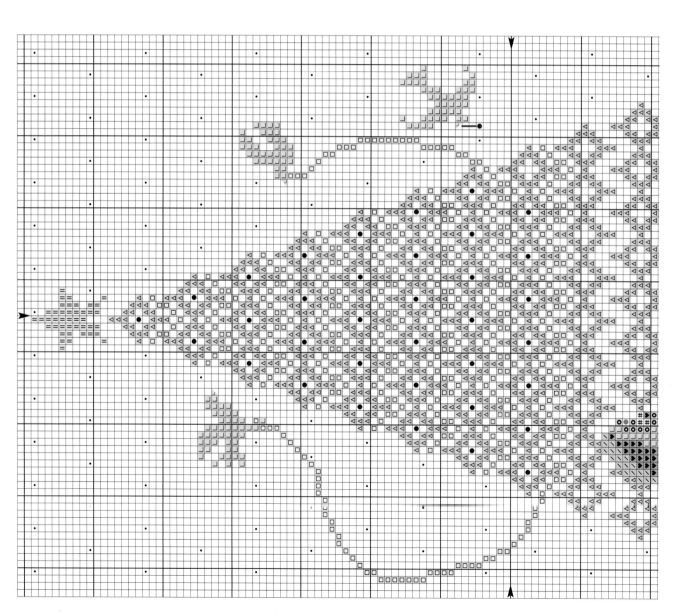

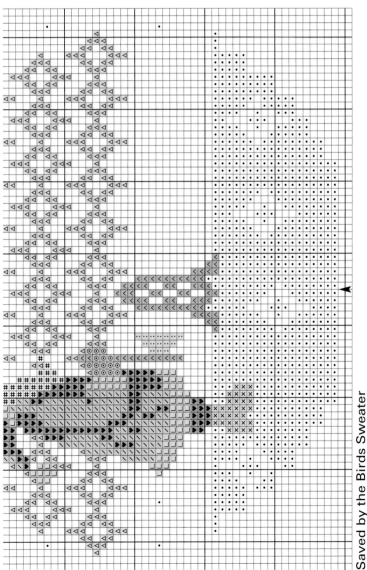

Saved by the Birds Sweater

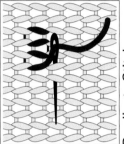

Duplicate Stitch

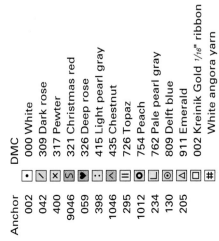

Saved by the Birds – Sleeve

Anchor	DMC	
002	•	000 White
042	/	309 Dark rose
400	X	317 Pewter
9046	S	321 Christmas red
059	►	326 Deep rose
398	∷	415 Light pearl gray
1046	◁	435 Chestnut
295	‖	726 Topaz
1012	◉	754 Peach
234	⌐	762 Pale pearl gray
130	⊙	809 Delft blue
205	△	911 Emerald
	□	002 Kreinik Gold 1/16" ribbon
	#	White angora yarn

STRAIGHT STITCH
9046 ╱ 321 Christmas red – bird
with ornament on
right side of sweater

Anchor	DMC	
		FRENCH KNOT
400	●	317 Pewter – Santa's eye (6X)
9046	●	321 Christmas red – tree ornaments (12X)

Sweater Front stitch count: 138 high x 74 wide

Sweater Front finished design sizes:
As pictured – 13⅞ x 7⅜ inches
14-count fabric – 9⅞ x 5¼ inches
16-count fabric – 8⅝ x 4⅝ inches

Sleeve stitch count: 75 high x 31 wide

Sleeve finished design sizes:
As pictured – 7½ x 3⅛ inches
14-count fabric – 5⅜ x 2¼ inches
16-count fabric – 4⅝ x 2 inches

CHICKADEE VEST
As shown on page 77.

Fabric and Thread
Purchased vest with inserts of
18-count natural brown linen
fabric
Cotton embroidery floss in the
colors listed in the key at *right*

Supplies
Needle

Instructions
Find the center of the patch chart and
the center of the square vest insert;
begin stitching there. Use three plies of
floss to work the cross-stitches over
two threads of the fabric. Work the
backstitches using two plies of floss.
Work the French knots using two plies
of floss wrapped once around the needle. Stitch the vest strip chart in the
same manner. Press the finished vest
carefully from the back.

CHICKADEE VEST

Anchor		DMC	
002	·	000	White
403	■	310	Black
218	−	319	Dark pistachio
1025	/	347	Deep salmon
217	O	367	Medium pistachio
214	*	368	Light pistachio
862	▲	520	Deep olive drab
859	◉	523	Medium olive drab
851	X	924	Deep gray-blue
850	L	926	Medium gray-blue
848	∧	927	Light gray-blue
274	‖	928	Pale gray-blue
887	#	3046	Yellow-beige
847	⊟	3072	Beaver gray
382	●	3371	Black-brown
1023	♡	3712	Medium salmon
779	⊙	3768	Dark gray-blue

BACKSTITCH

403	/	310 Black – chickadees' eyes
382	/	3371 Black-brown – all remaining backstitches

FRENCH KNOT

382	●	3371 Black-brown – holly berries

Chickadee Patch stitch count: 42 high x 43 wide
Chickadee Patch finished design sizes:
18-count fabric – 2 1/3 x 2 1/3 inches
28-count fabric – 3 x 3 1/8 inches
36-count fabric – 2 3/8 x 2 3/8 inches
Chickadee Strip stitch count: 46 high x 92 wide
Chickadee Strip finished design sizes:
18-count fabric – 2 1/2 x 5 1/8 inches
28-count fabric – 3 1/4 x 6 5/8 inches
36-count fabric – 2 5/8 x 5 1/8 inches

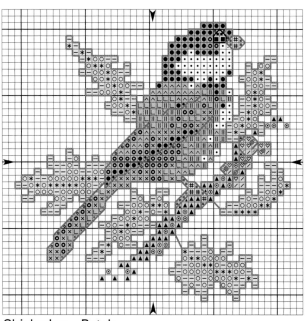

Chickadee – Patch

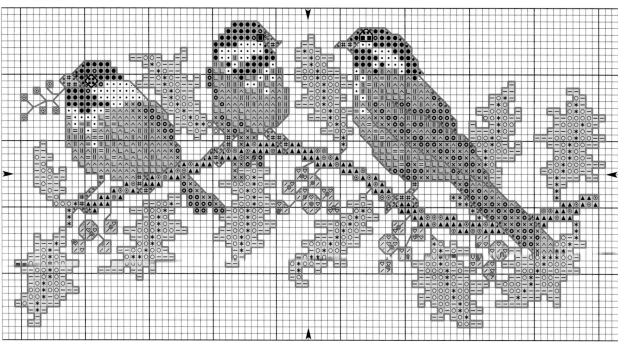

Chickadee – Strip

CHRISTMAS LIGHTS BLOUSE

As shown on page 78.

Fabric and Thread
Purchased blouse with a 1½×11½"
front placket of 28-count even-
weave fabric or plain blouse and
a 4×14" piece of 28-count Jubilee
to match blouse
Cotton embroidery floss in the
colors listed in the key on
page 86

Supplies
Needle
Sewing thread to match plain blouse

Instructions
Open the placket facing so you can
stitch only the top layer. Centering
the design, *pages 86–87,* use three
plies of floss to work the cross-stitches over two threads of the fabric.
Work the backstitches using one ply
of floss. Press the finished stitchery
carefully from the back. Fold the
placket facing back into position and
press. Baste the placket closed before
washing the blouse.

To add a placket to a plain blouse,
serge or zigzag-stitch the edges of the
fabric to prevent raveling. Find the
top stitch of the chart; measure ½"
from the top of the Jubilee fabric and
¾" from the left side; begin stitching
there. Stitch as directed above. Press
the finished stitchery carefully from
the back.

Press the top edge under even with
the top stitch; then fold the fabric in
half lengthwise and wrong sides
together to form a band. Position the
band over the button holes with the
top edge aligned with the seam at the
bottom of collar or collar band of the
blouse and the fold on the outer edge
of the blouse front. Fold at least ½" of
the bottom edge to the wrong side.
Make sure the fold does not intersect
with any of the buttonholes. (The
band should end at least ½" above or
below the nearest buttonhole because
the Jubilee and blouse will be stitched
together along this fold later.) Press
the fold and trim folded fabric to ½"
if necessary. Baste ½" from the long
edges. Pin the band to the blouse with
the stitched side against the right side
of the blouse and the basting line 1½"
from the front edge. Machine-stitch

along the basting line. Press the
band over the buttonholes. Topstitch
through all layers close to the top
and bottom folds.

HO-HO-HO APRON

As shown on page 79.

Fabric and Thread
15" length of 4"-wide White
16-count Aida banding
Purchased 20×28" red-and-green
plaid cotton towel
Cotton embroidery floss in the
colors listed in the key on
page 87
DMC metallic gold spooled
embroidery thread

Supplies
Needle
Erasable fabric marking pen
Sewing thread to match fabrics
2¾ yards of ⅝"-wide green
grosgrain ribbon
4—¾"-diameter red buttons

Instructions
Zigzag-stitch or overcast the ends of
the banding to prevent fraying. Find
the center of the chart, *pages 86–87,*
and the center of the banding; begin
stitching there. Use two plies of
floss to work the cross-stitches.
Work the blended-needle stitches as
specified in the key. Use one ply of
floss to work the backstitches. Work
the French knots using one ply of
floss wrapped once around the needle. Work the couching stitches as
specified in the key. Press the banding carefully from the back. Set the
banding aside.

At one short edge of the towel
(top of finished apron), measure
and mark the points 4" from each
corner with the erasable fabric
marking pen. On both long edges,
measure and mark the points that
are 10" from the same corners.
Connect the two marks on each
corner with a curving line (see
diagram, *right*). Cut away the excess
fabric along the marked lines.
Turn the cut edges under ¼" twice;
machine-topstitch.

Pin the top edge of the banding
1½" from the top edge of the towel.
Trim the banding ends ½" beyond
the edges of the towel; fold them

under. Machine-topstitch through
all layers close to all four edges of
the banding.

For the neck strap, cut a 26"
length of grosgrain ribbon. Fold the
ends of the ribbon under 1¼".
Position one folded ribbon end,
short side down, ½" from one edge
of the apron top. Place a button atop
the ribbon; sew through all layers of
fabric to secure. Fasten the other
end of the ribbon to the other side of
the apron top.

For the ties, cut the remaining ribbon into two equal lengths. Fold and
attach one piece in the same manner
as the neck strap to each of the corners at the bottom of the curved line.

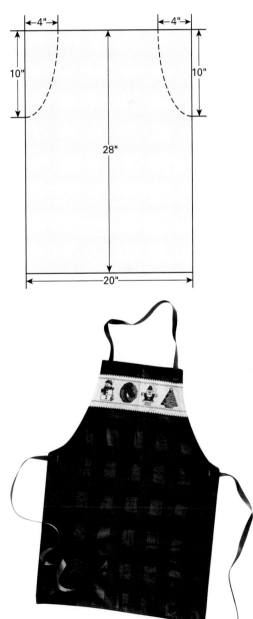

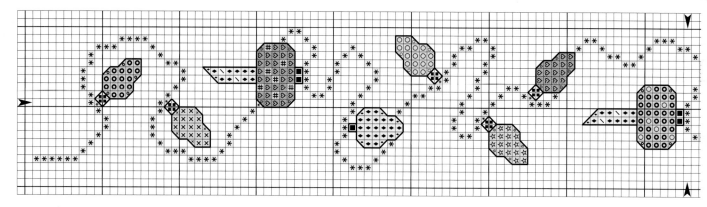

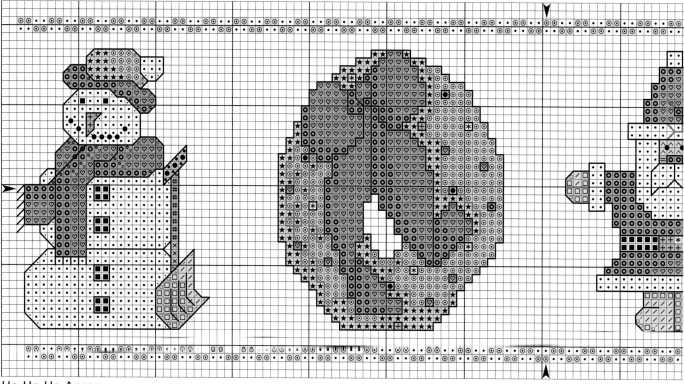

Ho-Ho-Ho Apron

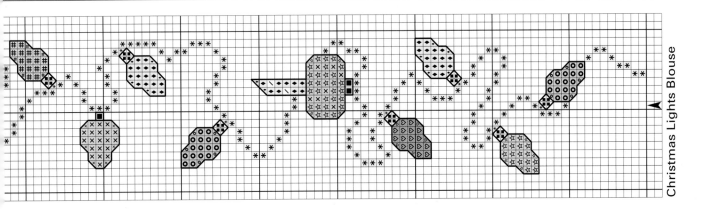

CHRISTMAS LIGHTS BLOUSE

Anchor		DMC
403	■	310 Black
046	◹	666 Red
901	✳	680 Old gold
209	○	912 Emerald
433	✕	996 Electric blue
035	#	3801 Watermelon
177	☆	3807 Cornflower blue
189	●	3812 Aqua
306	◆	3820 Straw
386	╱	3823 Yellow

BACKSTITCH

403		310 Black

Stitch count: 170 high x 18 wide
Finished design sizes:
28-count fabric – 12⅛ x 1¼ inches

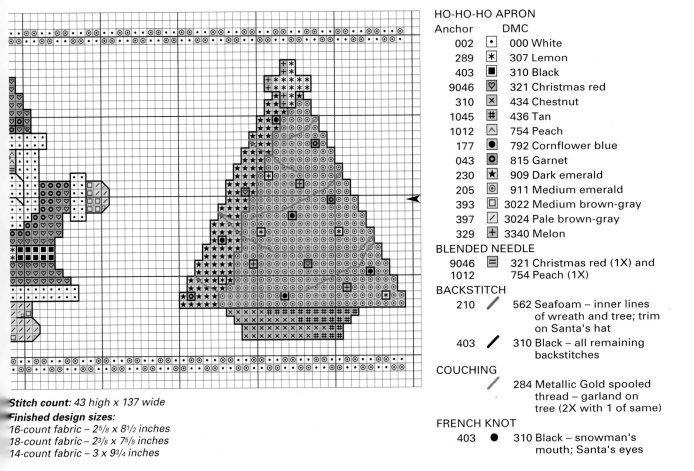

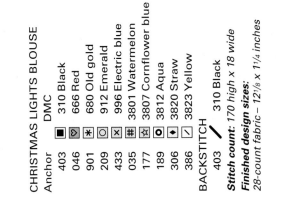

HO-HO-HO APRON

Anchor		DMC
002	•	000 White
289	✳	307 Lemon
403	■	310 Black
9046	♡	321 Christmas red
310	✕	434 Chestnut
1045	#	436 Tan
1012	∧	754 Peach
177	●	792 Cornflower blue
043	◉	815 Garnet
230	★	909 Dark emerald
205	◎	911 Medium emerald
393	□	3022 Medium brown-gray
397	╱	3024 Pale brown-gray
329	+	3340 Melon

BLENDED NEEDLE

9046	▤	321 Christmas red (1X) and
1012		754 Peach (1X)

BACKSTITCH

210	╱	562 Seafoam – inner lines of wreath and tree; trim on Santa's hat
403	╱	310 Black – all remaining backstitches

COUCHING

	╱	284 Metallic Gold spooled thread – garland on tree (2X with 1 of same)

FRENCH KNOT

403	●	310 Black – snowman's mouth; Santa's eyes

Stitch count: 43 high x 137 wide
Finished design sizes:
16-count fabric – 2⅝ x 8½ inches
18-count fabric – 2⅜ x 7⅝ inches
14-count fabric – 3 x 9¾ inches

STITCHED
for Giving

A unique aura surrounds a
handmade gift—love and warm
thoughts seem to emanate from the
stitches. No wonder each one
becomes the object of "oohs and
aahs" when it's unwrapped. From a
plush silk-ribbon embroidered robe
to a lacy Hardanger doily and doll
apron, we've selected some special
treasures for you to stitch and
share with those you love.

STITCHED FOR GIVING

Graced on both the front and back covers with a spray of small flowers stitched on silk gauze, the tiny antique notebook, left, *inspired the beautiful holiday gifts* below and opposite. *The colors of the wild roses on the front were brightened and stitched in their original size for a petite pin and matching earrings. On our notebook, the blue carnations from the back of the original were enlarged by working over two threads on 36-count linen and surrounded by lace to reflect its style. Instructions for both projects are on* pages 95–96.

Designs: Adapted from an antique

A touch of lace complements any romantic setting. This delicate Hardanger doily, worked in the traditional Norwegian technique, features tulip motifs and dove's eye openwork. Complete instructions begin on page 96.

With a classic chenille bathrobe and a week-end to stitch, you can produce the pretty and practical gift, opposite, for someone special. The flowers are worked in shades of lilac, periwinkle, rose, and burgundy silk ribbon with leaves of turquoise and aqua. Complete instructions begin on page 97.

Designs: Hardanger doily, Lynn Hermanson; Robe, De Selby

Doll collectors—from little girls to grandmothers—will appreciate this dainty pulled-thread apron. The lacy technique consists of eyelet, satin, and four-sided stitches, each gently tugged to open a tiny space in the fabric. Complete instructions begin on page 97.

Design: Rosemary Drysdale

STITCHED FOR GIVING

WILD-ROSE JEWELRY

As shown on page 90, finished pin measures 1¼" in diameter; earrings measure 1".

Fabric and Thread

2½×3½" piece of 32-count silk gauze mounted in cardboard mat
Silk thread in the colors listed in the key *below*

Supplies

Needle
4×4" piece of white broadcloth
Pencil
1—1⅛"-diameter (size 45) flat button form
2—⅞"-diameter (size 36) flat button forms
12" of ⅛"-wide gold braid
Crafts glue
Earring backs
Pin back
Wire cutters
Fine sandpaper
All-purpose cement

Instructions

To fit the pin and both earrings onto the gauze with adequate allowance for finishing, follow the placement instructions carefully. Designate one 2½" edge as the top of the gauze and mark it on the cardboard mat. For the pin, find the center of the chart. Find the horizontal center of the gauze and measure ⅝" from the right edge of the gauze; begin stitching there. Use one ply of silk thread to work half cross-stitches over one thread of gauze. Run thread under back side of stitches to avoid carrying thread across unstitched areas of the gauze.

For the first earring, find the center of the chart. Measure ½" from top edge of gauze and ½" from the left edge; begin stitching there. For the second earring, find the center of the chart again; measure ½" from bottom edge and from left edge; begin stitching there.

When all three motifs are stitched, turn the gauze over and remove the tape to separate the gauze from the mat.

From the broadcloth, cut one 1⅞" circle and two 1⅝" circles. Center the larger circle on the pin motif and the smaller ones on the earring motifs. Trace around each circle and cut them out. Center each gauze circle, right side up, on top of its respective broadcloth circle. Baste each pair of circles together using running stitches ¼" from the cut edge. Place the button form behind the broadcloth and pull the thread to smooth the fabric around each button form. Finish assembling the button following manufacturer's instructions. Beginning at the top of each button, glue the braid around the outer edge, overlapping the cut ends and gluing them to the back.

Use wire cutters to remove the button shanks. Sand the center back of each button form. Use all-purpose cement to glue the pin and earring backs in place.

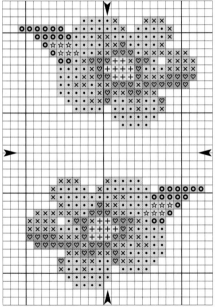

Wild-Rose Earrings

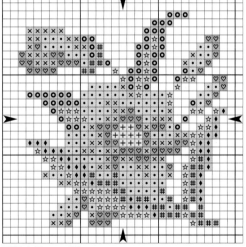

Wild-Rose Pin

WILD-ROSE JEWELRY
Kreinik Soie d'Alger Silk Floss
- • 3012 Light pink
- × 3014G Rose
- ♡ 2924A Red
- ◎ 2214T Olive
- ☆ 2124S Yellow-green
- ⊞ 2126N Dark green
- ◆ 245G Gray-green
- ⊞ 523G Gold

Earrings stitch count: 14 high x 23 wide
Earrings finished design sizes:
32-count fabric – ⅜ x ¾ inches
28-count fabric – ½ x ¾ inches
36-count fabric – ⅜ x ⅝ inches

Pin stitch count: 27 high x 27 wide
Pin finished design sizes:
32-count fabric – ⅞ x ⅞ inches
28-count fabric – 1 x 1 inches
36-count fabric – ¾ x ¾ inches

BLUE CARNATIONS NOTEBOOK

As shown on page 91, finished notebook is 3×5".

Fabric and Thread

10×12" piece of 36-count antique white linen

Silk thread in the colors listed in the key, *below*

Supplies

Needle
Needlework frame
22-ply paper chipboard
Crafts knife
Ruler
3×5" pad of white paper with rubber-bound edge
Strip of nylon hosiery
Drill with ³⁄₁₆" bit
Fusible interfacing
Paper-backed fusible adhesive
½ yard of ½"-wide scalloped rayon lace
Fabric glue
White felt
⅝ yard of ½"-wide blue organza ribbon
Large crewel needle

Instructions

Zigzag-stitch or overcast the edges of the fabric to prevent fraying. Sew a basting line 5" from and parallel to the 10" side. Find the center of the chart and the center of the remaining portion of fabric. Begin stitching there. Use two plies of floss to work the cross-stitches over two threads of fabric. Press the finished stitchery carefully from the back; set aside.

Use a crafts knife to cut one 3×5" rectangle for the book front and one 3×6⅛" rectangle for the back from the chipboard. With the crafts knife and ruler, score the front ½" from one short side, cutting just deep enough to allow the cardboard to bend at a right angle. Score the back in the same manner ⅜" from one short side and again ½" from the first scoring.

From fusible interfacing cut a 4×5½" rectangle and a 4×7" rectangle. Lay the first piece of interfacing on the scored side of the book front, aligning one short side with the side near the scored line and centering the long sides. Use an iron to fuse. Turn excess interfacing to back side and fuse, mitering corners. Center the

second interfacing rectangle on the scored side of the back; fuse. Turn excess interfacing to back side and fuse, mitering corners.

Lay the back on a flat surface, scored side down. Remove the cardboard back from the pad of paper, if present. Lay the pad on the back, aligning the binding with the inner scored line. Lay the book front on top of the pad with scored line at the same end as those of the back. Fold the back along the scored lines over the pad, bringing the ⅜" flap over the book front. On the ⅜" flap, mark positions for two holes, each centered left to right and about ¾" from the long sides of the book. Tie the nylon strip firmly around the book to hold the flap and the paper pad in position and drill through all the layers (flap, front, pad, and back). Cut the nylon, remove the paper pad, and set it aside.

To cover front, trim the stitched linen 2" beyond stitching on each side and 1¼" inches at top and bottom. From remaining linen, cut a 7⅛×4" piece to cover the back, avoiding zigzag-stitching or overcasting. Cut fusible adhesive in the same sizes. Working on a terrycloth towel, fuse the adhesive to the back side of the same-size pieces of linen, being careful to avoid the stitched area of the front. Remove the paper backing and lay the linen front, right side up, on the covered side of the book front, aligning the left short side with the side near the scored line and centering the long

sides. Fuse, avoiding stitching. Fold excess fabric to the back side and fuse, trimming and mitering corners. Remove the paper backing, center the linen back on the covered side of the book back, and fuse. Fold excess fabric to the back side and fuse in the same manner as the front.

Glue the lace around the stitched design on the three unscored sides of the front. Cut two 3×5" rectangles of white felt and glue to the inside covers. Reassemble the book as directed for the drilling step. Using the crewel needle and starting from the front, thread the ribbon through one hole, across the back, and through the remaining hole. Tie the ends in a double bow and trim.

HARDANGER DOILY

As shown on page 92, the finished doily measures 9⅜×9⅜ inches.

Fabric and Thread

16×16" piece of 20-count Light tan Jobelan fabric
2 skeins of Ecru #8 pearl cotton
1 ball of Ecru #5 pearl cotton
1 skein of DMC 644 Light beige-gray #8 pearl cotton
1 ball of DMC 644 Light beige-gray #5 pearl cotton

Supplies

Needle

Instructions

Zigzag-stitch or overcast the edges of the fabric to prevent fraying. Find

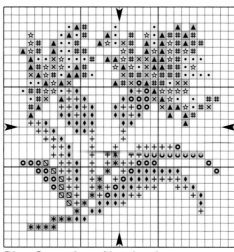

Blue Carnations Notebook

BLUE CARNATIONS NOTEBOOK
Kreinik Soie d'Alger Silk Floss

·	5053 Light blue
☆	1442S Medium blue
#	1444T Blue
▲	1423T Dark blue
✕	3742G Tan
+	2124S Yellow-green
◆	2126N Dark green
⊠	245G Gray-green
⊍	2214T Olive
✳	4115G Brown

Stitch count: 26 high x 26 wide
Finished design sizes:
36-count fabric – 1½ x 1½ inches
28-count fabric – 1⅞ x 1⅞ inches
32-count fabric – 1⅝ x 1⅝ inches

the Kloster block at the top center of the chart, *page 99*. Find the vertical center of the fabric and measure 1¾" from the edges; begin stitching there. Use one strand of #5 pearl cotton to work the Kloster blocks, other satin stitches, and buttonhole stitches over the number of threads indicated on the chart (see diagrams, *page 98*). Use one strand of #5 pearl cotton to work the backstitches. Refer to the diagram, *page 98,* and use one strand of #8 pearl cotton to work the Algerian eyelets over four threads of the fabric. Give each stitch a gentle tug to open a small hole in the center.

Referring to the Removing threads diagram on *page 98,* cut and remove the threads for the openwork areas.

For split wrapped bars with dove's eye, use #8 pearl cotton and refer to the diagrams on *page 98*. Wrap the pearl cotton around two threads of fabric until three sides of the square are wrapped (count Kloster blocks as wrapped sides). On the fourth side, wrap about halfway, then weave the dove's eye, passing the needle under the satin stitches of Kloster blocks and around woven bars. Complete wrapping the fourth bar.

Carefully trim away the excess fabric close to the buttonhole stitches. Press the finished doily carefully from the back.

RIBBON-EMBROIDERED ROBE
As shown on page 93.

Fabric and Thread
Purchased chenille bathrobe with a
    shawl collar
Light turquoise #3 pearl cotton
    (DMC 597)
YLI silk ribbon in the colors and
    sizes listed in the key on
    page 101

Supplies
Tear-away stabilizer
Fine-tip permanent black
    marking pen
Needle
White and terra-cotta sewing thread
4—¼"-diameter white buttons

Instructions
Use the permanent marking pen to transfer the patterns on *page 101* onto

the tear-away stabilizer. Baste the appropriate pattern to each side of the robe collar. Referring to the diagram on page *100*, use one strand of pearl cotton to work the feather stitches. Work the Japanese-leaf stitches, the lazy-daisy stitches, and the French knots using one strand of ribbon and referring to the diagrams on *page 100.*

For the folded rose, follow the instructions in the tip box on *page 100,* using a 10" length of ribbon.

For the folded roses with ruffle, cut a 6" length of 13 mm ribbon. Work a gathering thread along one long edge of the ribbon. Tighten the thread to make a 1¼" disc shape. Sew the gathered ribbon to the appropriate position on the robe. Then construct a folded rose using a 10" length of ribbon and tack it to the center of the gathered ribbon. Sew the buttons in positions indicated on the chart. Remove the basting threads and carefully tear away the stabilizer, making sure no stitches are pulled loose.

PULLED-THREAD DOLL APRON
As shown on page 94, finished apron fits an 18" doll.

Fabric and Thread
17×9" piece of 28-count White
    Cashel linen
White #12 pearl cotton

Supplies
Needle
Needlework frame
Basting thread
1¼ yards of white double-fold
    bias tape

Instructions
For pulled thread, give every stitch a gentle tug to open a hole in the linen, unless otherwise specified. All stitches are worked with pearl cotton. Begin each new thread with a waste knot (see *page 124*).

Zigzag-stitch or overcast the edges of the fabric to prevent fraying. For the skirt, find the arrow on the chart, *page 102,* and measure 5½" from the top and 1" from the left edge of fabric. Work the entire first eyelet (eight legs or straight

stitches into the center) there. Then, count 16 threads above the eyelet and begin working the diagonal rows of eyelets, referring to the Diagonal Star Eyelet diagram, *page 103* (work four legs of each eyelet as you work diagonally downward and the remaining four legs as you return to the starting point of each row).

Work the rows of pulled satin stitch above and below the eyelets. Work last four-sided stitch row.

For mosaic filling stitch, refer to the diagram, *page 103,* work a square with four pulled satin stitches on each side. Work a four-sided stitch in the center of each square and a cross-stitch inside the four-sided stitch. (For a neat back, begin stitching at the right left and work the stitches in diagonal rows, satin-stitching on the downward trip and completing the four-sided stitch and cross-stitch on the return trip.) Work the second horizontal row of four-sided stitches.

For square-edge hemstitch, begin stitching four threads to the left of end of the top row of pulled satin stitches and four threads above the gathering line indicated on the chart. Referring to the diagrams, *page 103,* work the three-sided stitch around three edges of the skirt. *Do not* pull the three-sided stitches. Before working the wrapped backstitches at the upper right corner of the skirt, fold the raw edge of the fabric at the right edge of the skirt to the back along the vertical line formed by the three-sided stitches. Working through both layers and referring to the diagram, use the last three-sided stitch as a guide to work a double backstitch over four threads (needle and thread should end on the wrong side); pull tightly. Wrap the thread over the fold and work the second double backstitch in the next three-sided stitch; pull tightly. Continue to within four stitches of the corner. Fold the bottom edge of the apron to the back and stitch through four layers of fabric for at least four stitches before and after turning the corner. Continue working around the skirt to upper left corner. Turn the piece over and trim excess fabric close to the backstitches. Continue cutting as *Continued* needed above the gathering line to remove the skirt piece the fabric.

For the bib, find the mosaic filling stitch indicated by the arrow on the chart and measure 1" from the left and 1" from the bottom edge of the remaining fabric; begin stitching there, working in diagonal rows. Work square-edge hemstitch on all four sides and trim.

Press both pieces carefully. Hand- or machine-stitch a line of gathers along the line indicated on the chart.

Pull threads and gather to measure 4½". Cut a 21" piece of bias tape, unfold and press each short end under ¼". Center the tape on the gathered apron, right sides together, with one outer fold of the tape on the gathering line. Baste and hand- or machine-stitch. Trim away excess linen. Refold the bias tape, forming ties from the unstitched ends and covering the raw edge of the linen; pin. Slip-stitch the folded edges of one tie together; then slip-stitch the

fold of the bias tape to the back of the apron. Slip-stitch the remaining folded edges together.

Center and baste the bottom edge of the bib on the skirt, so it just covers the bias tape. Sew securely in place along the backstitch row of hemstitches. Cut two 10" pieces of bias tape. Unfold the tape and press the short ends under ¼". Refold tape and slip-stitch the folded edges together. Sew one end of each tie to one upper corner of the bib.

Hardanger Pointers

Hardanger's lacy patterns have been stitched in Norway for hundreds of years, but it almost became a lost art in the early 20th century. While stitchers recognize the beauty and enjoy the rhythm of Hardanger stitching, they often hesitate to cut threads for the delicate open patterns. The cutting doesn't have to be intimidating, even for first-time stitchers. With a little caution, some practice, and these special tips it's easy to create an heirloom.

1. Stitch all of the Kloster blocks and any other stitches that adjoin the cut sections before you begin cutting threads. Their function is to keep cut threads from fraying. Be sure the Kloster blocks are aligned directly across from each other.
2. Be at your best when you try the first cut. Avoid cutting fabric threads when you're tired. Make sure you have adequate light for cutting. Use a magnifier, if you have one.
3. Choose scissors with very fine blades. Some stitchers like scissors with a hook on the bottom blade (Lift 'n' Snips is one brand).
4. Always cut perpendicular to the Kloster block (see Removing threads diagram, *right*).
5. Beginners may want to cut one thread at a time. Insert the tip of the bottom scissor blade under the fabric thread(s) and return the tip to the surface before you actually make the cut.
6. If you do accidentally cut threads parallel to—instead of perpendicular to—the Kloster block, you can repair the problem like this: Remove the miscut threads. Loosen a fabric thread at the edge, pull it out, and thread into a needle. Secure the thread by weaving the end through the back of the Kloster block satin stitches. Then, following the weave of the fabric, weave through the Kloster block outward to the opposite Kloster block. Referring to the diagram at right, turn and repeat the steps until all cut threads have been replaced.

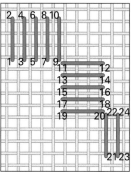

Kloster Block

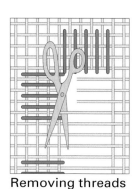

Removing threads

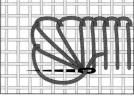

Buttonhole Stitch

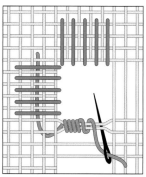

Split Wrapped Bars

Algerian Eyelet

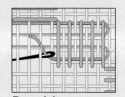

Repairing
Cutting Error

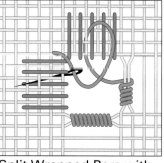

Split Wrapped Bars with
Dove's Eye

Hardanger Doily

HARDANGER DOILY
BACKSTITCH
／ 644 Beige-gray #5 pearl cotton

SATIN STITCH
Ecru #5 pearl cotton

BUTTONHOLE STITCH
Ecru #5 pearl cotton

KLOSTER BLOCKS
Ecru #5 pearl cotton

ALGERIAN EYELETS (16 legs over 4)
644 Beige-gray #8 pearl cotton

SPLIT WRAPPED BARS
Ecru #8 pearl cotton

DOVE'S EYE
Ecru #8 pearl cotton

Stitch count: 94 high x 94 wide
Finished design sizes:
20-count fabric – 9³/₈ x 9³/₈ inches
28-count fabric – 6³/₄ x 6³/₄ inches

Japanese-Leaf Stitch

Feather Stitch

Lazy Daisy

French Knot

Folded Rose

Thread a needle with thread that matches your ribbon; set aside. Fold the center of the ribbon at a 45-degree angle (see Figure 1). Fold end B of the ribbon to the right over the first fold (see Figure 2). Fold end A of the ribbon up over the previous fold of the ribbon (see Figure 3).

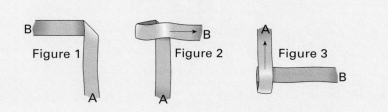

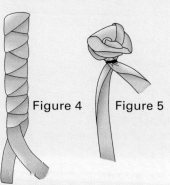

   The folds will form a square shape. Continue to make folds until all of the ribbon is used. Grasp the ribbon ends in one hand, and release the folds; the ribbon will spring up in accordion folds (see Figure 4). Holding one ribbon end, gently pull down the other end until you form a rose (see Figure 5).

   Using matching sewing thread, sew twice through the center of the rose. Sew back and forth through the base of the rose several times until the petals are secure, catching the ends as you stitch. Trim the excess ribbon. Hand-sew it in place.

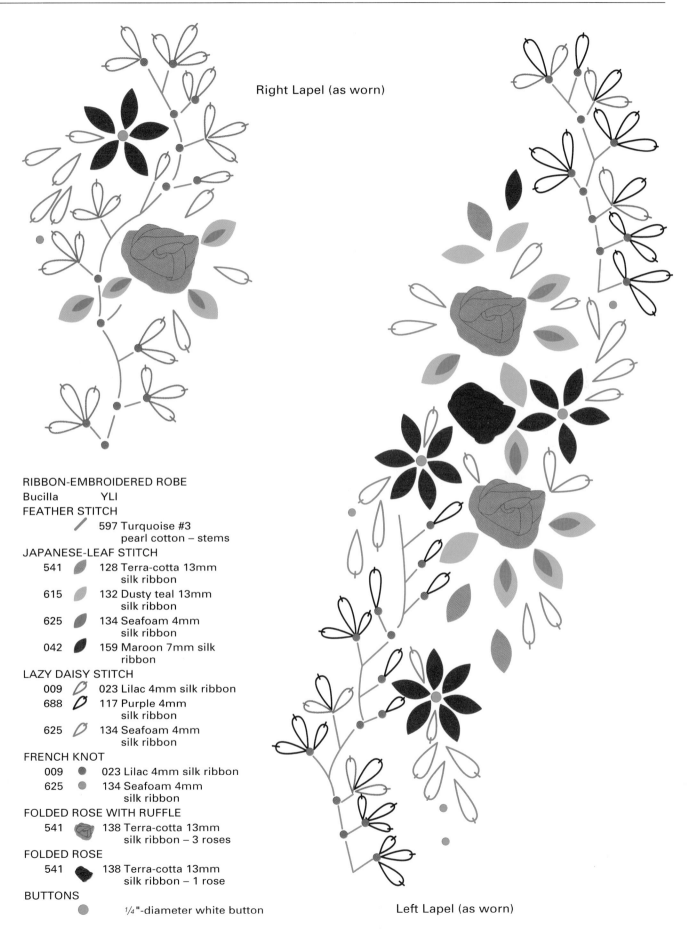

Right Lapel (as worn)

RIBBON-EMBROIDERED ROBE

Bucilla   YLI

FEATHER STITCH

597 Turquoise #3
pearl cotton – stems

JAPANESE-LEAF STITCH

541   128 Terra-cotta 13mm
silk ribbon

615   132 Dusty teal 13mm
silk ribbon

625   134 Seafoam 4mm
silk ribbon

042   159 Maroon 7mm silk
ribbon

LAZY DAISY STITCH

009   023 Lilac 4mm silk ribbon

688   117 Purple 4mm
silk ribbon

625   134 Seafoam 4mm
silk ribbon

FRENCH KNOT

009   023 Lilac 4mm silk ribbon

625   134 Seafoam 4mm
silk ribbon

FOLDED ROSE WITH RUFFLE

541   138 Terra-cotta 13mm
silk ribbon – 3 roses

FOLDED ROSE

541   138 Terra-cotta 13mm
silk ribbon – 1 rose

BUTTONS

¼"-diameter white button

Left Lapel (as worn)

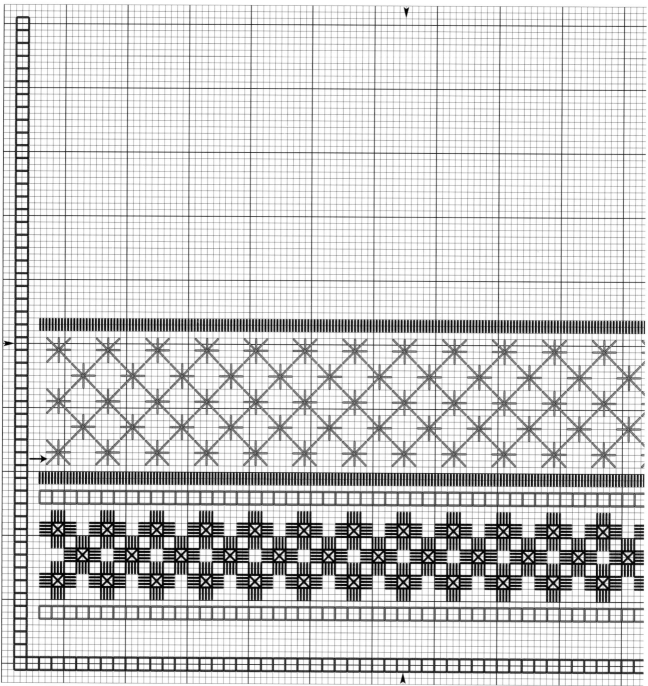

Apron Skirt

DOLL APRON

DMC
SQUARE EDGE HEMSTITCH
000 White #12 pearl cotton –
bib, skirt

MOSAIC FILLING STITCH
000 White #12 pearl cotton –
bib, band 5 on skirt

PULLED SATIN STITCH
000 White #12 pearl cotton –
bands 2 and 3 on skirt

DMC
FOUR SIDED STITCH (over 2)
000 White #12 pearl cotton –
bands 4 and 6 on skirt

STAR EYELET
000 White #12 pearl cotton –
band 1 on skirt

Apron Bib stitch count: 42 high x 42 wide
Apron Bib finished design sizes:
28-count fabric – 3 x 3 inches
32-count fabric – 2⅝ x 2⅝ inches
36-count fabric – 2⅓ x 2⅓ inches

Apron Skirt stitch count: 92 high x 122 wide
Apron Skirt finished design sizes:
28-count fabric – 6½ x 8¾ inches
32-count fabric – 5¾ x 7⅝ inches
36-count fabric – 5 x 6¾ inches

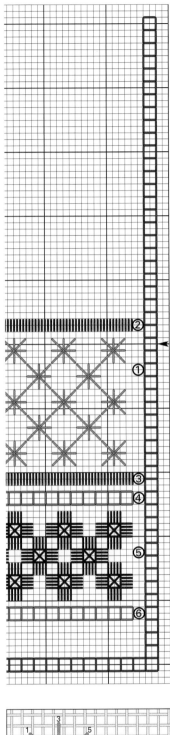

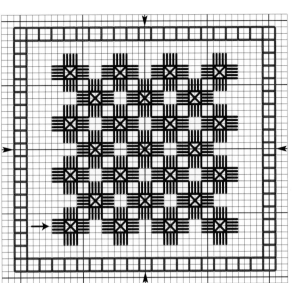

Apron Bib

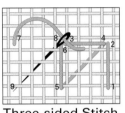

Three-sided Stitch
Square-Edge Hemstitch

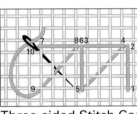

Three-sided Stitch Corner

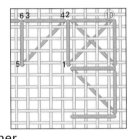

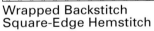

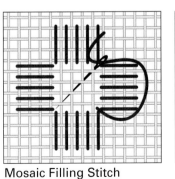

Wrapped Backstitch
Square-Edge Hemstitch

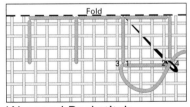

Mosaic Filling Stitch

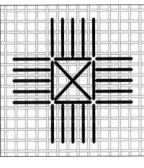

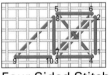

Four-Sided Stitch

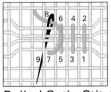

Pulled Satin Stitch

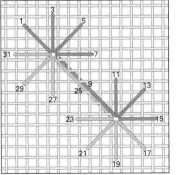

Star Eyelet (worked on the diagonal)

Christmas
CHARACTERS

Enliven your holiday

decor with familiar

personalities from

favorite Christmas

legends and stories.

Santas, snowmen, angels,

and elves are but a few

of the characters

in this collection. Stitch

these festive figures

to brighten the season

in your home or to

share as gifts.

Dozens of elves help Santa prepare for his big night; your home should have some helpers on hand too! This artistic imp, above, *welcomes holiday guests. He's finished as a wall quilt with strip-pieced borders and candy cane buttons. Your guests will also love these nutcrackers,* opposite, *the stern-faced soldiers and kings that Tchaikovsky immortalized as Christmas symbols. Both the Tula place mats and the perforated paper figures (sandwiched between clear glass plates and brass chargers) are easy to finish. Instructions begin on* page 108.

Designs: Elf, De Selby; Nutcrackers, Phyllis Dobbs

CHRISTMAS CHARACTERS

Add some winter cheer to any holiday setting with wintry personalities. The gentle gift-giver, opposite, *is only one of the many personas of Santa Claus. The light blue 14-count Aida background and sparkly metallic braid set the frosty moonlit mood of this classic piece. The perfect proportions of the roly-poly snow family* below *were achieved by stitching each design on a different count of Aida or Hardanger fabric. Each figure has separate charts for front and back. Complete instructions for both projects begin on* page 114.

Designs: Santa, Carol Rodgers; Snow Family, Robin Clark

CHRISTMAS CHARACTERS

The season abounds with symbols of peace and joy—angels, reindeer, and doves. These satiny figures are stitched on sparkly fabric with rayon floss for a distinctively elegant touch. Finish them as ornaments for your own tree or enclose each one in a precut card as a special greeting. For a home decor gift, the card becomes a mat that fits in a standard frame. Turn to page 120 for complete instructions.

Designs: Barbara Sestok

PAINTING CHRISTMAS MERRY QUILT
As shown on page 104, the finished quilt measures 17½×19¼".

Fabric and Thread
16×20" piece of 28-count Sage Jobelan fabric
⅝ yard of 45"-wide light-green print fabric
¼ yard each of 45"-wide dark-green print and red print fabric
⅛ yard of 45"-wide gold print fabric
20×20" piece of cotton batting
Cotton embroidery floss in the colors listed in the key on *page 111*
Metallic gold embroidery floss

Supplies
Needle
Needlework frame
Sewing thread to match fabrics
Quilter's ruler, rotary cutter, and mat or air-soluble quilt marker

Thread for quilting
Four 1¼"-tall candy cane buttons

Instructions
Zigzag-stitch or overcast the edges of the fabric to prevent fraying. Find the center of the chart, *pages 110–111,* and the center of the fabric; begin stitching there. Use three plies of cotton or metallic floss to work the cross-stitches over two threads of the fabric. Work the French knots using one ply of floss wrapped once around the needle. Work the backstitches using one ply of floss. Use four plies of floss to work the straight stitches over the number of threads indicated. Press the finished stitchery from the back. Centering the design, trim the fabric to measure 12" high and 14" wide.

From the light-green fabric, cut four 1¼×22" sashing strips, four 2½×45" binding strips, and one

20×20" quilt back. From both the dark-green and the red fabric, cut four 2½×22" striped-sashing strips. From the gold fabric, cut four 2½×2½" corner squares. All seams are sewn with the right sides together unless otherwise specified in the instructions. Measurements include ¼" seam allowances.

Sew a 1¼"-wide light-green sashing strip to the top and bottom edge of the Jobelan. Press the seam allowances toward the sashing. Trim the ends of the sashing even with side edges of the Jobelan. Then, sew a 1¼" light-green sashing strip to each side of the stitched Jobelan fabric. Press the seam allowances toward the sashing. Trim the ends even with the top and bottom; set the quilt top aside.

To make the striped sashing, sew the long edges of the dark-green and red strips together alternating the

colors (see the diagram *below*). Press the seams open. Starting at one corner of the joined strips, use the ruler and a rotary cutter to cut across the strip at a 45-degree angle. Rotary-cut parallel to the first cut to make four 2½"-wide striped sashing strips as shown in the diagram. *(Or, use an air-soluble marker to draw diagonal lines on the fabric. Cut along the lines with scissors.)*

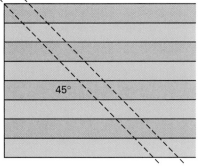

Striped Sashing

Trim two of the striped-sashing strips to the same length as the sides of the quilt top (about 13"). Sew a gold corner square to both ends of each strip. Press the seam allowances toward the corners. Set the strips aside.

Sew one of the remaining striped-sashing strips to the top of the stitched piece and the other to the bottom. Press the seam allowances toward the center. Trim the ends of the strips even with the sides of the quilt top. Sew the striped sashing with gold corners to the sides of the quilt top, matching the corner seams to the horizontal seam between the two pieces of sashing. Press the seam allowance toward the center.

Place the quilt back, right side down, on a smooth surface. Center and smooth the batting on the back. Center the pieced quilt top on the batting; baste through all layers.

Hand- or machine-quilt in the ditch (on the seam lines) along the horizontal and vertical seams of the sashing pieces. Trim away the excess back fabric and batting even with the edges of the sashing.

Sew the short ends of the binding strips together and press the seam open. Fold the binding strip in half lengthwise, wrong sides together and press. Press one end of the binding strip under ½" and align the raw edges of the binding with the edge of the front. Pin and stitch the binding to the quilt top, mitering the corners. Turn the folded edge of the binding to the back and slip-stitch to the seam line. Sew a button in the center of each gold square.

Painting Christmas Merry

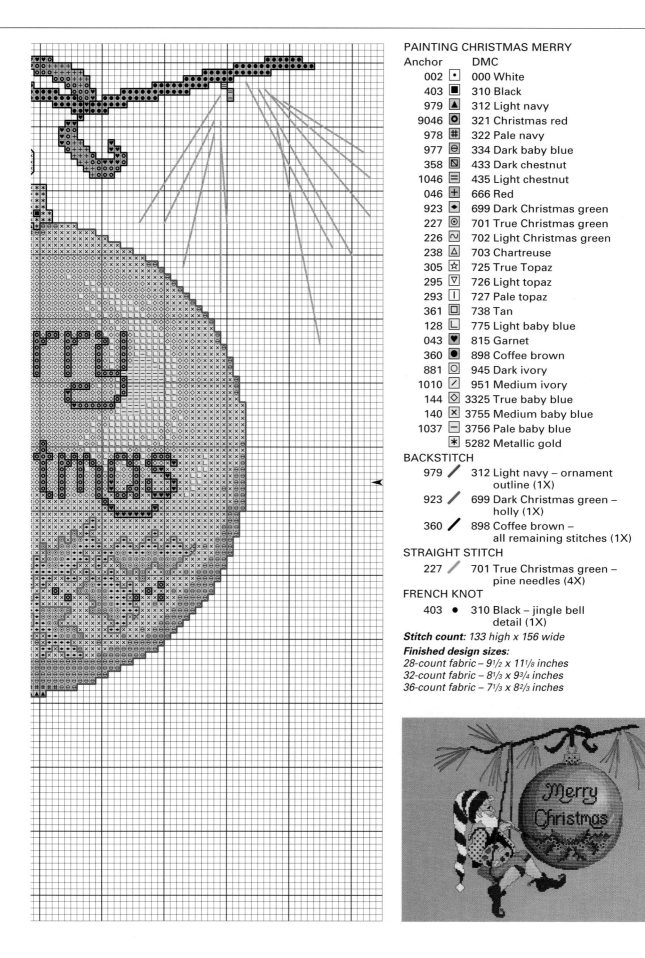

PAINTING CHRISTMAS MERRY

Anchor		DMC	
002	·	000	White
403	■	310	Black
979	▲	312	Light navy
9046	◉	321	Christmas red
978	⊞	322	Pale navy
977	⊖	334	Dark baby blue
358	◩	433	Dark chestnut
1046	=	435	Light chestnut
046	+	666	Red
923	◆	699	Dark Christmas green
227	⊙	701	True Christmas green
226	～	702	Light Christmas green
238	△	703	Chartreuse
305	☆	725	True Topaz
295	▽	726	Light topaz
293	Ɪ	727	Pale topaz
361	▢	738	Tan
128	L	775	Light baby blue
043	♥	815	Garnet
360	●	898	Coffee brown
881	○	945	Dark ivory
1010	/	951	Medium ivory
144	◇	3325	True baby blue
140	✕	3755	Medium baby blue
1037	–	3756	Pale baby blue
	✳	5282	Metallic gold

BACKSTITCH

979	╱	312 Light navy – ornament outline (1X)
923	╱	699 Dark Christmas green – holly (1X)
360	╱	898 Coffee brown – all remaining stitches (1X)

STRAIGHT STITCH

227	╱	701 True Christmas green – pine needles (4X)

FRENCH KNOT

403	●	310 Black – jingle bell detail (1X)

Stitch count: 133 high x 156 wide

Finished design sizes:
28-count fabric – 9½ x 11⅛ inches
32-count fabric – 8⅓ x 9¾ inches
36-count fabric – 7⅓ x 8⅔ inches

NUTCRACKER PLACE MATS

As shown on page 105, the finished place mats measure 12×18".

Fabric and Thread
4—12×18" pieces of 10-count White Tula fabric
Cotton embroidery floss in the colors listed in the key, *opposite*
One additional skein each of White, 310, 666, and 798
DMC 5282 metallic gold floss

Supplies
Needle
Needlework frame
6 yards of ⅜"-wide metallic gold flat braid trim
White and gold sewing thread

Instructions
Use white sewing thread to machine-topstitch around each piece of fabric ⅜" from the edge. With a long edge at the top, measure 2¾" from the right edge and 2¼" from the bottom of the place mat; begin stitching the bottom row of the nutcracker's boot there. Use four plies of floss to work the cross-stitches. Work the backstitches using two plies of floss. Position the gold trim ⅞" from the edge of the fabric. Machine-topstitch over the braid with gold sewing thread. For fringe, carefully remove the Tula threads between the cut edge and the white topstitching.

NUTCRACKER PAPER FIGURES

As shown on page 105.

Fabric and Thread
For each figure
3×7" piece of 14-count White perforated paper
Cotton embroidery floss in the colors listed in the key, *opposite*
DMC 5282 metallic gold floss

Supplies
Needle
Scissors

Instructions
Find the center of the desired nutcracker chart and the center of the perforated paper; begin stitching there. Use two plies of floss to work the cross-stitches. Work the backstitches using one ply of floss. Cut out the shape one square beyond the stitched area of the design.

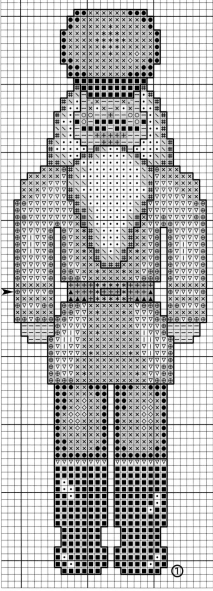

Nutcracker Place Mats
and Paper Figures

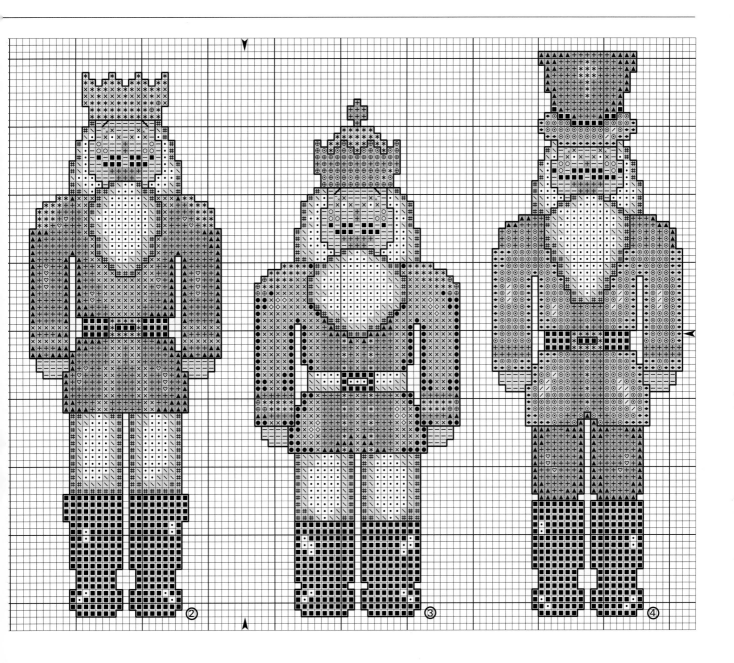

NUTCRACKER PLACE MATS AND PAPER FIGURES

Anchor		DMC
002	·	000 White
403	■	310 Black
399	⊞	318 Steel
398	\	415 Pearl gray
212	◆	561 Dark seafoam
210	⊙	562 Medium seafoam
206	/	564 Light seafoam
046	+	666 Red
302	▽	743 True yellow
300	‖	745 Light yellow
307	⊕	783 Christmas gold
133	●	796 Royal blue
131	⊠	798 Dark Delft blue
130	◇	809 True Delft blue

Anchor		DMC
1005	▲	816 Garnet
881	–	945 Ivory
060	⊙	3688 Mauve
033	♡	3706 Watermelon
	✴	5282 Metallic gold

BACKSTITCH
403	/	310 Black – all stitches

Nutcracker #1 stitch count: *82 high x 29 wide*
Nutcracker #1 finished design sizes:
10-count fabric – 8 1/4 x 3 inches
14-count fabric – 5 7/8 x 2 inches
Nutcracker #2 stitch count: *80 high x 29 wide*
Nutcracker #2 finished design sizes:
10-count fabric – 8 x 3 inches
14-count fabric – 5 3/4 x 2 inches
Nutcracker #3 stitch count: *76 high x 31 wide*
Nutcracker #3 finished design sizes:
10-count fabric – 7 5/8 x 3 inches
14-count fabric – 5 3/8 x 2 1/4 inches
Nutcracker #4 stitch count: *82 high x 29 wide*
Nutcracker #4 finished design sizes:
10-count fabric – 8 1/4 x 3 inches
14-count fabric – 5 7/8 x 2 inches

SANTA AND REINDEER
As shown on page 106.

Fabric and Thread
12×14" piece of 14-count Light blue Aida cloth
Cotton embroidery floss in the colors listed in the key, *right*
Kreinik #8 braid in the colors listed in the key, *right*

Supplies
Needle
Needlework frame
Desired mat and frame

Instructions
Zigzag-stitch or overcast the edges of the fabric to prevent fraying. Find the center of the chart and the center of the fabric; begin stitching there. Use three plies of floss or one strand of braid to work the cross-stitches. Work the backstitches using one ply of floss. Press the finished stitchery carefully from the back. Mat and frame the piece as desired.

ROLY-POLY SNOW FAMILY
As shown on page 107.

Fabric and Thread
For the father
14" square piece of 14-count White Aida cloth
14" square piece of lightweight fusible interfacing
For the mother
12" square piece of 18-count White Aida cloth
12" square piece of lightweight fusible interfacing
For the baby
10" square piece of 22-count White Hardanger fabric
10" square piece of lightweight fusible interfacing
Cotton embroidery floss in the colors listed in the key on *page 116*

Supplies
Basting thread
Needle
Needlework frame
Matching sewing thread
Plastic pellets
Polyester fiberfill

Instructions
For each figure, zigzag-stitch or overcast the edges of the fabric to prevent fraying. Divide the fabric into four rectangles by folding the fabric in half crosswise and basting along the fold. Then, unfold and refold in thirds in the opposite direction; baste along one of the fold lines. Find the center of the appropriate front chart, *pages 116–117,* and the center of one large rectangle; begin stitching there.

For the 14-count Aida cloth, use three plies of floss to work the cross-stitches. Use two plies of floss to work the cross-stitches on the 18-count and 22-count fabrics. Work the backstitches using one ply of floss. Work the French knots using one ply of floss wrapped once around the needle. Stitch the back chart in the same manner on the remaining large rectangle. Use the small rectangles to stitch the base chart four times. Press the finished stitchery carefully from the back.

Remove the basting. Fuse the interfacing to the back of the stitched fabric following the manufacturer's instructions. Machine-stay-stitch around each shape close to the cross-stitches. Cut out each shape ½" beyond the stay stitching. Pin the front to the back with right sides together and raw edges even. Machine-stitch around the side and top edges of the figure, following the outline of the design, and leaving the bottom straight edge unstitched and an opening in the middle of one side for turning. Trim the seam and clip the curves; *do not* turn. Set the figure aside.

For the base, sew the straight edges of base sections together in pairs. Trim the seams and press open. Sew the straight edges of the joined base sections together. Trim the seams and press open.

Matching each side seam of the figure to a base seam, pin the base to the bottom edges of the figure. Machine-stitch along the stay stitching around the edges of the base. Trim the seams, clip the curves, and turn right side out through the opening in the side. Fill the base of the figure with plastic pellets; firmly stuff the rest of the figure with fiberfill. Hand-sew the opening closed.

SANTA AND REINDEER

Anchor		DMC	
002	·	000	White
403	■	310	Black
148	●	311	True navy
979	✕	312	Light navy
235	▦	414	Steel
398	◹	415	Pearl gray
358	▲	433	Dark chestnut
310	◉	434	Medium chestnut
1045	▢	436	Tan
1005	◓	498	Christmas red
832	▤	612	Medium drab brown
831	▽	613	Light drab brown
923	◆	699	Dark Christmas green
227	▽	701	True Christmas green
024	○	776	Pink
045	♥	814	Dark garnet
043	✚	815	Medium garnet
1011	▬	948	Peach
1031	◈	3753	Antique blue
1037	⟋	3756	Pale baby blue
1009	▯	3770	Ivory
778	△	3774	Rose-beige
1050	◆	3781	Dark mocha
899	△	3782	Light mocha
393	◩	3790	Beige-gray
	⊕	001	Kreinik Metallic silver #8 braid
	✳	002	Kreinik Metallic gold #8 braid

BACKSTITCH
| 140 | ╱ | 3755 | Medium baby blue – snow |
| 403 | ╱ | 310 | Black – all remaining stitches |

Stitch count: 134 high x 85 wide
Finished design sizes:
14-count fabric – 9½ x 6 inches
16-count fabric – 8⅓ x 5⅓ inches
18-count fabric – 7⅜ x 4¾ inches

Santa and Reindeer

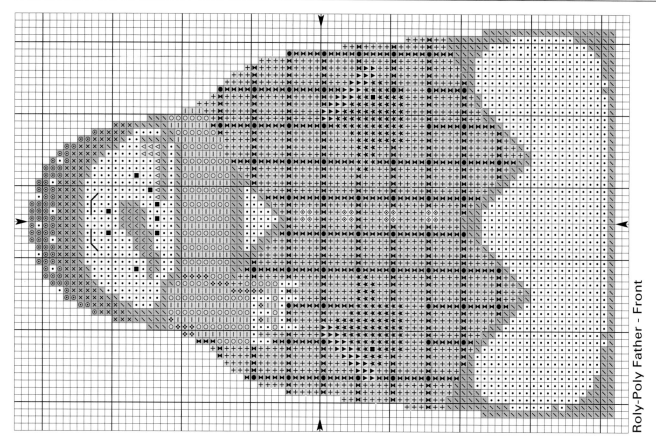

Roly-Poly Father - Front

ROLY-POLY SNOW FAMILY

Anchor	DMC	
002	·	000 White
897	⋈	221 Shell pink
403	■	310 Black
1025	★	347 Salmon
1005	▶	498 Christmas red
683	✢	500 Deep blue-green
878	▮	501 Dark blue-green
875	◯	503 True blue-green
859	⊕	523 Olive drab
891	✳	676 Light old gold
886	⧖	677 Pale old gold
890	◈	729 Medium old gold
897	●	902 Garnet
1035	△	930 Dark antique blue
1034	▶	931 Medium antique blue
1033	▨	932 True antique blue
862	+	934 Pine green
397	◉	3024 Brown-gray
903	▷	3032 Medium mocha
1032	◁	3752 Light antique blue
1048	◿	3776 Mahogany
1050	✕	3781 Dark mocha

Anchor	DMC	
	BACKSTITCH	
403	╱	310 Black – father's eyebrows and bell on hat and tassel on baby's hat
683	╱	500 Deep blue-green – squares on mother's scarf and collar and waistband on baby's sweater
886	╱	677 Pale old gold – plaid of father's coat
360	╱	3031 Deep mocha – tail of father's hat
	FRENCH KNOT	
403	●	310 Black – bell on father's hat

Roly-Poly Father stitch count: *84 high x 54 wide*
Roly-Poly Father finished design sizes:
14-count fabric – 6 x 3⅞ inches
Roly-Poly Mother stitch count: *84 high x 54 wide*
Roly-Poly Mother finished design sizes:
18-count fabric – 4⅝ x 3 inches
Roly-Poly Baby stitch count: *84 high x 54 wide*
Roly-Poly Baby finished design sizes:
22-count fabric – 3¾ x 2½ inches

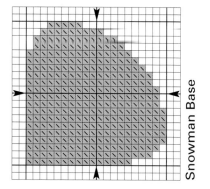

Snowman Base

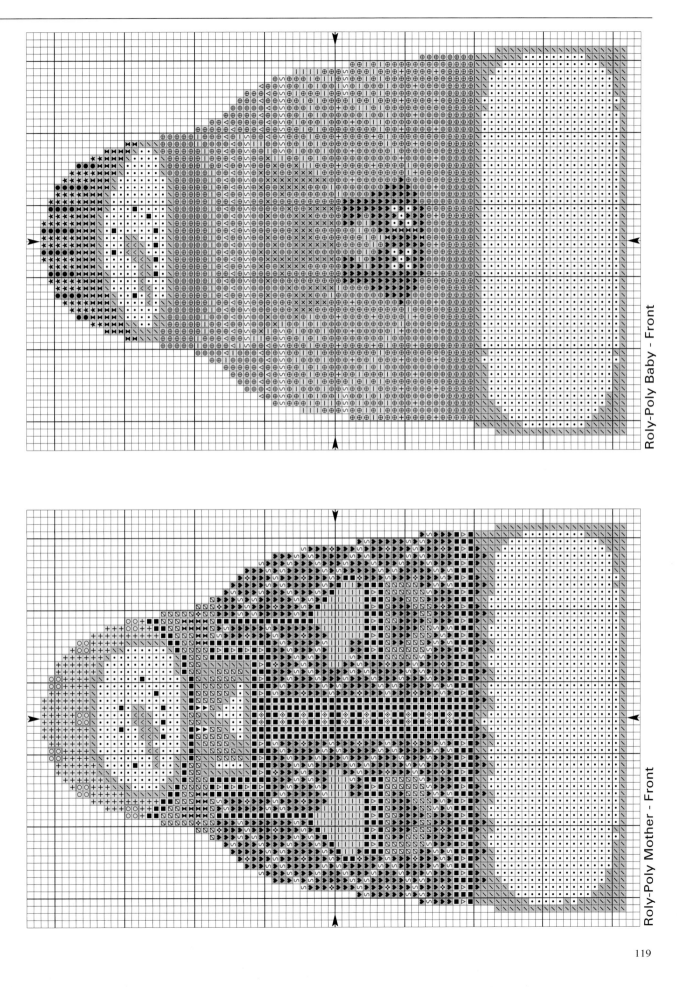

Roly-Poly Baby - Front

Roly-Poly Mother - Front

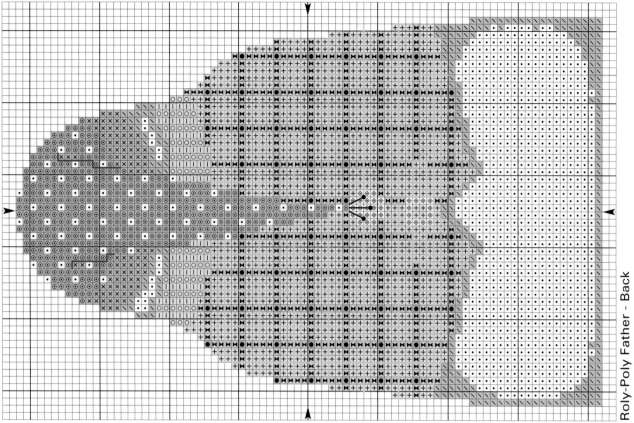

Roly-Poly Father - Back

ROLY-POLY SNOW FAMILY

Anchor	DMC		
002		000	White
897		221	Shell pink
403		310	Black
1025		347	Salmon
1005		498	Christmas red
683		500	Deep blue-green
878		501	Dark blue-green
875		503	True blue-green
859		523	Olive drab
891		676	Light old gold
886		677	Pale old gold
890		729	Medium old gold
897		902	Garnet
1035		930	Dark antique blue
1034		931	Medium antique blue
1033		932	True antique blue
862		934	Fine green
397		3024	Brown-gray
903		3032	Medium mocha
1032		3752	Light antique blue
1048		3776	Mahogany
1050		3781	Dark mocha

Anchor	DMC	
BACKSTITCH		
403	310	Black – father's eyebrows and bell on hat and tassel on baby's hat
683	500	Deep blue-green – squares on mother's scarf and collar and waistband on baby's sweater
886	677	Pale old gold – plaid of father's coat
360	3031	Deep mocha – tail of father's hat
FRENCH KNOT		
403	310	Black – bell on father's hat

Roly-Poly Father stitch count: *84 high x 54 wide*
Roly-Poly Father finished design sizes:
14-count fabric – 6 x 3⅞ inches
Roly-Poly Mother stitch count: *84 high x 54 wide*
Roly-Poly Mother finished design sizes:
18-count fabric – 4⅝ x 3 inches
Roly-Poly Baby stitch count: *84 high x 54 wide*
Roly-Poly Baby finished design sizes:
22-count fabric – 3¾ x 2½ inches

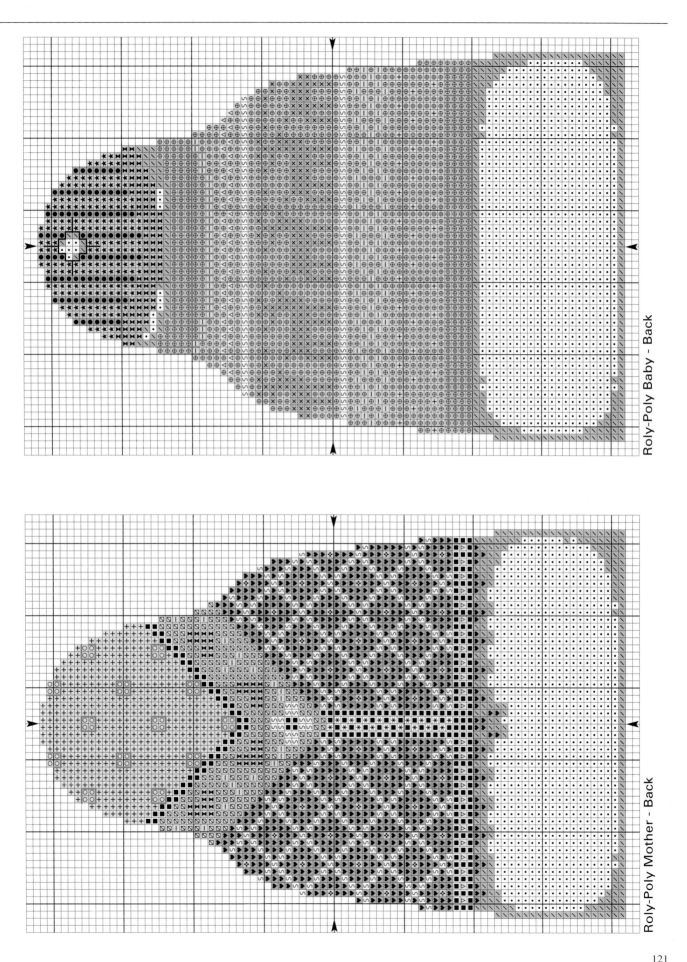

Roly-Poly Baby - Back

Roly-Poly Mother - Back

ANGEL, DOVE, AND REINDEER ORNAMENTS
As shown on pages 108–109.

Fabric and Thread
For each ornament
6×8" piece of 28-count White-and-silver or Cream-and-gold Quaker cloth
4½×6" piece of fusible fleece
Rayon embroidery floss in the colors listed in the key *below*
Mill Hill 02006 Ice blue seed beads

Supplies
Needle
Tracing paper
Crafts glue
Masking tape
For the ornament
15½" piece of ¼"-wide metallic gold flat trim
4½×6" piece each of lightweight cardboard and ivory felt
5" piece of gold cord (optional)

For the card
Purchased 5×7" blue card with a 3½×5" oval opening
Snowflake-motif rubber stamp
Stamp pad
Silver embossing powder
Electric-heat tool, hot plate, or toaster
For the framed piece
Purchased 5×7" green card with a 3½×5" oval opening
Purchased 5×7" gold frame

Instructions
Zigzag-stitch or overcast the edges of the fabric to prevent fraying. Find the center of the chart and the center of the fabric; begin stitching there. Use two plies of rayon floss to work the cross-stitches over two threads of the fabric. Work the backstitches using one ply of floss. Use two plies of floss to work the straight stitches. Work the French knots using one ply of floss wrapped twice around the needle. Use two plies of floss to work the lazy daisy stitches. Attach the seed beads to the centers of the stars using one ply of matching floss. Place the finished stitchery facedown on a soft towel and carefully press from the back.

For all the designs, make an oval pattern by tracing the oval opening of the card; cut out. (*Or, fold a piece of tracing paper 3½×5" or larger into quarters and trace the pattern, below. Cut on the traced line and unfold.*) Use the paper pattern to cut an oval shape from the fusible fleece. Centering the design, fuse the oval to the back of the finished stitchery following the manufacturer's instructions.

For the ornament, cut out the fabric ¼" beyond the edge of the fleece oval. Use the paper pattern to cut oval shapes from the felt and the cardboard. Glue the stitched ornament to the cardboard, folding excess fabric to the back. Beginning at the top of the ornament, glue the

---

ANGEL, DOVE, AND REINDEER ORNAMENTS

Marlitt		DMC Rayon	
839	●	30301	Mahogany
831	♡	30351	Coral
830		30352	Light coral
1030	✕	30471	Avocado green
1209	⦶	30498	Dark Christmas red
893	⬚	30666	Bright Christmas red
1078	S	30676	Old gold
852	△	30702	Green
1036	✱	30739	Tan
1001	∧	30754	Peach
1059	L	30800	Delft blue
1072	◆	30839	Beige-brown
853	⊕	30895	Hunter green
1072	▲	30898	Coffee brown
1009	◪	30931	Antique blue
821	◩	30972	Canary
869	⊞	30976	Golden brown
800	⦂	35200	Snow white

BACKSTITCH

843	/	30321	Christmas red – reindeer harness and blanket
838	/	30336	Navy blue – dove
1209	/	30498	Dark Christmas red – berries on angel dress
844	/	30814	Garnet – ribbon
1040	/	30839	Beige-brown – holly leaves and angel
1072	/	33371	Black-brown – strings on mandolin and reindeer

Marlitt		DMC Rayon	
STRAIGHT STITCH			
831	/	30351	Coral – angel's mouth
852	/	30702	Green – berry leaves on angel's hair
1059	/	33325	Baby blue – stars
FRENCH KNOT			
801	●	30310	Black – dove's eye
843	●	30321	Christmas red – reindeer harness
1209	●	30498	Dark Christmas red – berries
1040	●	30839	Beige-brown – mandolin
1072	●	33371	Black-brown – angel eyes
MILL HILL GLASS BEADS			
	●	02006	Ice blue – star centers

Angel stitch count: 43 high x 38 wide
Angel finished design sizes:
28-count fabric – 3 x 2¾ inches
32-count fabric – 2⅝ x 2⅜ inches
Reindeer stitch count: 48 high x 41 wide
Reindeer finished design sizes:
28-count fabric – 3⅜ x 3 inches
32-count fabric – 3 x 2½ inches
Dove stitch count: 44 high x 44 wide
Dove finished design sizes:
28-count fabric – 3⅛ x 3⅛ inches
32-count fabric – 2¾ x 2¾ inches

Fold

Angel, Dove, and Reindeer Ornament Oval Pattern

Fold

gold trim around the edge of the ornament. If desired, fold the gold cord in half to form a loop. Glue the cut ends to the back side of the cardboard at the top. Glue the felt to the back of the ornament.

To emboss the card, press the rubber stamp onto the ink pad. Position the stamp as desired on the card and press. Sprinkle the embossing powder over the freshly-stamped image before it dries. Turn the card over and tap it gently onto a piece of paper to remove the excess powder. (Pour the excess powder back into the bottle to use later.) Use an electric-heat tool or hold the card over a hot plate or toaster to melt the embossing powder.

Center the ornament or cross-stitch design within the card opening, trimming the fabric, if necessary to fit. Tape the stitchery to the inside of the card. If desired, place the card in a purchased frame.

Dove Ornament

Reindeer Ornament

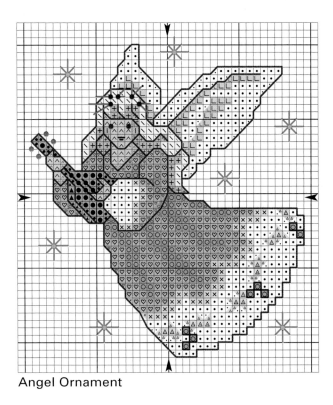

Angel Ornament

CROSS-STITCH BASICS AND SPECIAL STITCHES

Getting started

The written instructions for each project tell you where to begin stitching. For most projects the starting point is at the center. Every chart has arrows that indicate the horizontal and vertical centers. With your finger, trace along the grid to the point where the two centers meet. Compare a symbol at the center of the chart to the key and choose which floss color to stitch first. To find the center of the fabric, fold it into quarters and finger-crease or baste along the folds with a single ply of contrasting floss.

Cut the floss into 15" to 18" lengths, and separate all six plies. Recombine the plies as indicated in the project instructions, and thread them into a blunt-tip needle.

Basic cross-stitch

Make one cross-stitch for each symbol on the chart. For horizontal rows, stitch the first diagonal of each stitch in the row. Then work back across the row, completing each stitch. On most linen and even-weave fabrics, work your stitches over two threads as shown in the diagram *below*. For Aida cloth, each stitch fills one square.

You also can work cross-stitches in the reverse direction. Just remember to embroider the stitches uniformly—that is, always work the top half of each stitch in the same direction.

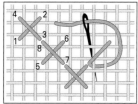

Cross-Stitch Worked Singly

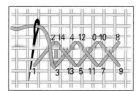

Cross-Stitch Worked in Rows

To secure thread at the beginning

The most common way to secure the beginning tail of the thread is to hold it under the first four or five stitches.

To secure the thread with a waste knot, thread the needle and knot the end of the thread. Insert the needle from the right side of fabric, about 4 inches away from the first stitch. Bring the needle up through the fabric, and work the first series of stitches. When finished, clip the knot on the right side. Rethread the needle with excess floss and push the needle through to the stitches on the wrong side of the fabric.

When you work with two, four, or six plies of floss, use a loop knot. Cut half as many plies of thread, but make each one twice as long. Recombine the plies, fold the strand in half, and thread all of the ends into the needle. Work the first diagonal of the first stitch, then slip the needle through the loop formed by folding the thread.

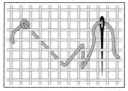

To Secure Thread at the Beginning

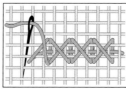

To Secure Thread with a Waste Knot

To secure thread at the end

To finish, slip the threaded needle under previously stitched threads on the wrong side of the fabric for four or five stitches, weaving the thread back and forth a few times. Clip the thread.

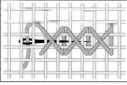

To Secure Thread at the End

Quarter and three-quarter cross-stitches

To obtain rounded shapes in a design, use quarter and three-quarter cross-stitches. On linen and even-weave fabrics, a quarter cross-stitch will extend from the corner to the center intersection of the threads. To make quarter cross-stitches on Aida cloth, estimate the center of the square. Three-quarter cross-stitches combine a quarter cross-stitch with a half cross-stitch. Both stitches may slant in any direction.

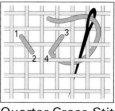

Quarter Cross-Stitch

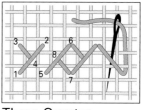

Three-Quarter Cross-Stitch

Algerian eyelet

The key to making this spoked stitch with its center hole is working from the outside in. Bring the needle from the back to the front at an outside edge of the stitch, then push it to the back at the midpoint of the stitch, pulling the thread firmly and gently. As you work successive spokes, an opening will appear in the middle.

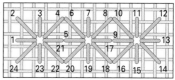

Algerian Eyelet

Backstitches

Backstitches define and outline the shapes in a design. For most projects, backstitches require only one ply of floss. On the color key, (2X)

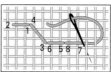

Backstitch

indicates two plies of floss, (3X) indicates three plies, etc.

Chain stitch

Bring the needle to the front of the fabric, and return to the back through the same hole, forming a loop. Slide the tip of the needle under two or more threads and then bring it to the front of the fabric. Slip the loop under the needle tip. Pull gently until the loop lies smoothly on the fabric. Pass the needle to the back, forming the loop of the second stitch of the chain.

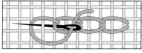
Chain Stitch

Couching

You'll need two needles to work a line of couching. Bring the heavier couched thread through the fabric at the beginning of the line designated on the chart and to the back at the end. Roughly align it in the position indicated on the chart. Bring the lighter couching thread through the fabric four threads (unless otherwise specified on chart) beyond the entry point of the couched thread, over it, and to the back in the next hole. Move four threads along the line of the couched thread, and repeat the couching. Continue along the entire length of the couched thread.

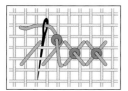
Couching

Cross-stitches with beads

When beads are attached using a cross-stitch, work the (first) half cross-stitches and then attach the beads on the return stitches.

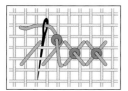
Cross-Stitches with Beads

French knot

Bring the threaded needle through the fabric, and wrap the floss around the needle as shown. Tighten the twists, and return the needle through the fabric in the same place. The floss will slide through the wrapped thread to make the knot.

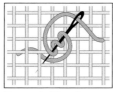
French Knot

Half cross-stitches

A half cross-stitch is half of a cross-stitch. They usually are listed under a separate heading in the color key and are indicated on the chart by a diagonal colored line.

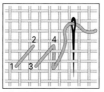
Half Cross-Stitch

Lazy-daisy stitch

Bring the needle to the front of the fabric, and return to the back through the same hole, forming a loop. Slide the tip of the needle under two or more threads, then bring it to the front of the fabric. Slip the loop under the needle tip. Pull gently until the loop lies smoothly on the fabric. Push the needle to the back, forming a tack stitch over the end of the loop.

Lazy-Daisy Stitch

Running stitch

Running stitches work up fast and add definition to a design. They are usually equal in length, but uneven stitches give a novelty effect.

Running Stitch

Satin stitch

This smooth-surface stitch may be worked over a few or many threads. Bring the needle up through the first hole. Count threads along a straight line, and return to the back of the fabric. For the second stitch, bring the needle up through the hole immediately next to the first stitch.

Satin Stitch

Smyrna cross-stitch

A Smyrna cross-stitch consists of an X-shaped stitch topped by a straight-horizontal stitch and a straight-vertical stitch. It's often worked over four, six, eight, or more threads.

Smyrna Cross-Stitch

Straight stitches

The simplest of all stitches, straight stitches often are used for sun rays, whiskers, and other simple accents.

Straight Stitch

FABRICS FOR CROSS-STITCH

Many stitchers like to work cross-stitch designs using fabrics and threads other than those specified in the projects. Here's helpful information for completing the projects in this book and adapting them to your own preferences.

Before you begin a project on a fabric other than that specified, stitch a small sample. Be sure you're happy with the amount of detail on the new fabric and the way the thread covers it. Also note whether the needle slips smoothly through the fabric.

Cross-stitch fabrics

Work counted cross-stitch on any fabric that lets you make consistently sized, even stitches. There are many fabrics marketed specifically for cross-stitch. Usually, they're interchangeable when the stitch-per-inch counts match. For example, a project that calls for 28-count linen stitched over two threads can easily be worked on 14-count Aida. A higher-count fabric will yield a smaller project. When a design is enlarged by working on lower-count fabric, some of the detail may be lost. Most of the charts in this book give you conversion information which tells you the size of the design when worked on other fabric counts.

Aida cloth is the most popular of all cross-stitch fabrics. The threads are woven in groups separated by tiny spaces. This creates a pattern of squares across the surface of the fabric and lets a beginning stitcher easily see where to place the cross-stitches. Measure Aida cloth by the number of squares per inch; for example, 14-count Aida cloth has 14 squares per inch. Look for Aida cloth in 6, 8, 11, 14, 16, and 18 thread counts. You'll find 14-count Aida cloth in more than 60 colors. For beginners, white Aida cloth is available with a removable grid of pre-basted threads.

Experienced stitchers consider linen to be the standard of excellence for cross-stitch fabric. The threads used to weave linen vary in thickness, giving the fabric a slightly irregular surface. Measure thread count by the number of threads per inch, but remember that because most designs are worked over two threads, 28-count linen will yield 14 stitches per inch. Linens are made in counts from 14 (seven stitches per inch) to 40.

The market for specialty fabrics for counted cross-stitch continues to grow with the popularity of the craft. These fabrics are referred to as even-weave fabrics because they're woven from threads with a consistent diameter, even though some of these fabrics have a homespun look. Count most even-weave fabrics like linen—by the number of threads per inch—and stitch over two threads.

Use Hardanger fabric for very fine counted cross-stitch. This traditional fabric for the Norwegian embroidery of the same name has an over-two, under-two weave that produces 22 small squares per inch.

Cross-stitch using waste canvas on clothing and other fabrics that aren't otherwise suitable for stitching. The canvas marks the squares and is designed to unravel when dampened after stitching is complete. It ranges in count from 6½ to 20 stitches per inch.

Cross-stitch charts can be worked 32- or 40-count silk gauze, 14-count perforated paper, 5- to 24-count needlepoint canvas, or even plastic canvas. These materials have no provision for fractional (quarter and three-quarter) stitches, so choose a chart with all whole stitches.

Threads for stitching

You can use most types of commercially available embroidery thread for counted cross-stitch projects.

Six-ply cotton embroidery floss comes in the widest range of colors, including variegated colors. It separates easily into single or multiple plies for stitching. The instructions with each project in this book tell you how many plies to use. If you use a different fabric, use the chart below right as a guide, and experiment on a scrap of the fabric until you achieve the desired effect. A greater number of plies will result in a dense or heavily textured piece; a smaller number of plies will create a lightweight or delicate texture.

Rayon and silk floss are similar in weight to six-ply cotton embroidery floss but have a higher sheen. Both can be interchanged with cotton floss, one ply for one ply, but because they have a "slicker" texture, you may find them more difficult to use.

You'll find pearl cotton available in four sizes: #3, #5, #8, and #12 (#3 is heavy; #12 is fine). It has an obvious twist and a high sheen.

Flower thread is a matte-finish cotton thread, available in about 180 colors. Substitute one strand of flower thread for two plies of floss.

A product currently available is overdyed thread. Most colors have an irregularly variegated, "one-of-a-kind" appearance. Cotton floss, silk floss, flower thread, and pearl cotton all are available in this form. All of them produce a soft, shaded appearance without changing thread colors.

Specialty threads add a distinctive look to cross-stitch work. They range in weight from hair-fine blending filament, usually used with floss, to ⅛-inch-wide ribbon. Specialty threads include numerous metallic threads, richly colored and textured threads, and fun-to-stitch, glow-in-the-dark threads.

Needle types

Blunt-tip needles work best on most cross-stitch fabrics because they slide through the holes and between threads without splitting or snagging the fibers. A large-eyed needle accommodates most threads. Many companies sell such needles labeled "cross-stitch," but they're identical to tapestry needles—blunt tipped and large eyed. The chart *below* will guide you to the right needle size for most common fabrics.

One exception to the blunt-tip needle rule is waste canvas; use a sharp embroidery needle to penetrate this fabric.

Working with seed beads requires a very fine needle that will slide through the holes. Two readily available options are a #8 quilting needle, which is short with a tiny eye, and a long beading needle which has a longer eye.

Fabric/Needles/Floss		
Fabric	Tapestry-Needle Size	Number of Plies
11-Count	24	Three
14-Count	24–26	Two
18-Count	26	Two
22-Count	26	One

INDEX

SOURCES

Many of the materials and items used in this book are available at crafts and needlework stores. For more information write or call the manufacturers listed below.

Fabrics: Charles Craft, P.O. Box 1049, Laurenburg, NC 28353. Wichelt Imports, Inc., Rte. 1, Stoddard, WI 54648. Zweigart, 2 Riverview Dr., Somerset, NJ 08873-1139, 732/271-1949.

Threads: Anchor, Consumer Service Dept., P.O. Box 27067, Greenville, NC 29616. DMC, Port Kearney Bldg. 10, South Kearney, NJ 07032-0650. Kreinik Manufacturing, Daisy Chain, P.O. Box 1258, Parkersburg, WV 26102.

Beads: Mill Hill, 800/447-1332.

Framing: Dot's Frame Shop, 4223 Fleur Dr., Des Moines, IA 50321.

Sample the Season

Page 13, Treats for a Sweet Season: Cream Brittney fabric—Zweigart.

Page 16, Village Santa: Bone Lugana fabric—Zweigart.

Nativity: Summerstraw linen—Wichelt Imports, Inc.

Woodcut Santa: Nordic blue linen—Wichelt Imports, Inc.

Carol Samplers: Sandstone linen—Wichelt Imports, Inc.; Waterlilies and Wildflowers overdyed threads—Caron Collection, 67 Poland St., Bridgeport, CT 06605, 203/381-9999.

At Home for Christmas

Page 34, Cardinal Afghan: Teresa Afghan—Zweigart.

Page 35, Folk-Art Stockings: Oatmeal and Horizon blue Rustico Aida cloth—Zweigart.

Page 38, Christmas Rose Towel Set: Red-and-gold Aida banding—Zweigart.

Page 39, Ribbons-and-Holly Table Runner: Christmas red Lugana fabric—Zweigart.

Page 43, Joy Pillow: Pillow—An Adam Original, 7471 Lamar St. S., Cottage Grove, MN 55916, 612/459-6793.

Sledding Mice Stocking and Box: White Brittney fabric—Wichelt Imports, Inc.; papier mâché box—Decorator & Craft Corp., 428 S. Zelta, Wichita, KS 67207, 316/685-6265.

Treasured Tree Trims

Page 58, Victorian Ornaments: Natural Lite Aida cloth—Wichelt Imports, Inc.

Page 61, Angel Tree Topper: Raw linen Cashel linen—Zweigart.

Page 64, Six-Gore Balls: China white linen—Wichelt Imports, Inc.; Cream Dublin linen—Wichelt Imports, Inc.

Page 65, Jewel-Tone Eggs: Ivory, silver-and white, and gold-and-white Aida cloth—Zweigart; overdyed floss—Needle Necessities, 14746 NE. 95th St., Redmond, WA 98052, 206/881-2161; charm kit—Mill Hill.

Page 66, Holiday Needle Rolls: White linen—Charles Craft; Marlitt rayon floss—Anchor; ribbon—Midori Inc., 1432 Elliott Ave., W, Seattle, WA 98119, 800/659-3049.

Page 68, Lighthearted Ornaments: Perforated paper—Yarn Tree Designs, 117 Alexander St., P.O. Box 724, Ames, IA 50010, 800/247-3952.

Page 71, Tea Rose Framed Stockings: Cherub pink linen—Wichelt Imports, Inc.

Tea Rose Mini Stockings: Ivory damask Aida cloth—Zweigart; Marlitt rayon floss—Anchor.

Dressed for the Holidays

Page 80, Snowman Jumpers: Jumpers—Rushwear, 800/257-7874.

Page 82, Saved by the Birds Duplicate-Stitch Sweater: Sweater—Lands' End, Lands' End Lane, Dodgeville, WI 53595-0041, 800/356-4444.

Page 84, Chickadee Vest: Vest—Sew Original, 6439 Ming Ave., Bakersfield, CA 93309, 805/832-9276.

Page 85, Christmas Lights Blouse: Blouse—Stitch-A-Blouse Blouse by Rushwear, Jubilee fabric—Zweigart.

Ho-Ho-Ho Apron: White banding—Zweigart.

Stitched for Giving

Page 95, Wild-Rose Jewelry: Silk Gauze and Soie d'Alger silk floss—Kreinik; button forms—Prym-Dritz Corp., P.O. Box 5028, Spartanburg, SC 29304.

Page 96, Blue Carnations Notebook: Antique white linen—Wichelt Imports, Inc.; Soie d'Alger silk floss—Kreinik; ribbon—Midori Inc.

Hardanger Doily: Light tan Jobelan fabric—Wichelt Imports, Inc.

Page 97, Ribbon-Embroidered Robe: Silk ribbon—YLI, 482 North Freedom Blvd., Provo, UT 84601; Bucilla, 1 Oak Ridge Rd., Humboldt Industrial Park, Hazelton, PA 18201.

Pulled-Thread Doll Apron: White Cashel linen—Zweigart; Kristen Larson doll—courtesy of Pleasant Company, for a free catalog call 800/845-0005.

Christmas Characters

Page 108, Painting Christmas Merry Quilt: Sage Jobelan fabric—Wichelt Imports, Inc.; metallic floss—DMC; Alma Lynne candy-cane buttons—Westwater Enterprises, 917 Mountain Ave., Mountainside, NJ 07092-2706, 908/654-8871.

Page 112, Nutcracker Place Mats: White Tula fabric—Wichelt Imports, Inc.; metallic gold flat braid—Wm. E. Wright, 85 South St., West Warren, MA 01092.

Nutcracker Paper Figures: Perforated paper—Yarn Tree Designs.

Page 114, Santa and Reindeer: Light blue Aida cloth—Zweigart.

Roly-Poly Snow Family: White Aida and Hardanger fabrics—Zweigart.

Page 120, Angel, Dove, and Reindeer Ornaments: White-and-silver and cream-and-gold Quaker cloth—Zweigart; Marlitt rayon floss—Anchor; cards—Yarn Tree Designs.

Photographs

Marcia Cameron: Pages 12 (top), 34, 36, 37, 38, 42, 63, 68, 71, 73, 81, 85, 90 (top), 114, 120.

Scott Little: Page 93.

Perry Struse: Cover and pages 6, 7, 8, 9, 10, 11, 12 (bottom), 26–27, 28, 29, 30, 31, 32, 33, 50–51, 52, 53, 54, 55, 56, 57, 74–75, 76, 77, 78, 79, 88–89, 90 (bottom), 91, 92, 93, 94, 100, 104–105, 106, 107, 108, 109, 110–111.

Steve Struse: Page 113.